Religious Psychology

P9-DGU-340

ALIENATION, ATHEISM AND THE RELIGIOUS CRISIS

ALIENATION, ATHEISM AND THE RELIGIOUS CRISIS

THOMAS F. O'DEA

SHEED AND WARD: NEW YORK

Library of Congress Catalog Card Number 69-19254

Manufactured in the United States of America

Contents

Contents

Introduction

We have become accustomed to speak of crisis and it must be conceded on all sides that it is just as well. For recognition of our present crisis, an attempt to confront and understand its many aspects, and serious effort to clarify and interpret our crisis experience in preparation for policy formation and action become immediate and pressing tasks. Despite their urgency, however, these are tasks not likely to be understood, let alone adequately carried out, in the near future. Becoming accustomed to crisis too often has simply made the condition livable, and enabled us to postpone or avoid serious confrontation of the challenge. We must however learn to combine tolerance and patience with serious and intelligent effort after understanding.

In our foreign and domestic policies as a nation the crisis reveals itself as a crisis of direction. What should we be doing with our enormous wealth and power? How should we use them to bring about the kind of world we desire? What kind of world indeed do we desire? Where shall we look to find an answer to that last question which shall embody the implications of the long

Western historical experience? The two institutional complexes most closely related to answering that final question, religion and education, are themselves in severe crises. I do not refer simply to the noisier aspects of that crisis, the defection of clergy, the campus disturbances, the resort to drugs nor even to the general malaise that spreads no one knows how far and in what covert and overt forms among our people. I refer rather to that deeper uncertainty of what we are and what we want to be which in a sometimes obscure and sometimes obvious way disorients us and distorts our comprehension of our contemporary predicament. That fundamental indecision which lies beneath both our shabbiest conventions and our profoundest acts of faith is the consequence of the new condition into which mankind is emerging in our day—a condition which harbors within itself both great promise and great threat.

This book is an attempt to speak of that crisis at its deepest root, of its religious aspects—the dilemmas of direction, of meaning, of values. It is this crisis which haunts Western Man in a variety of specific forms. Men in the past have generally lived in a condition that could be accurately characterized as community. They belonged to one socio-geographical entity; they shared a tradition with its explicit and implicit definition of values and its sense of direction; they recognized established authorities, however designated, as leaders and guides, and to some extent models, within the grounds as defined by the community and its tradition. This "community-tradition-authority" phenomenon has often been in crisis to one degree or another and in one place or another, but today we witness the advanced stages of its dissolution as a viable model of human society. The two great revolutions which we have experienced for nearly two centuries in the West and which have spread now in one form or another throughout the earth introduce as yet little understood qualitative changes in the character of human life.

The Industrial Revolution, itself perhaps in its early stages, has dissolved traditional community in the West and will do so in time throughout the world. This is not to overlook the tremendous difficulties facing the non-European peoples in their attempts to achieve economic growth as the basis for a modern society. Their success is indeed problematical for any predictable period ahead, but whatever the outcome, traditional societies as they existed in the 19th century are passing from the scene. The democratic revolution, certainly still in its initial stages, has destroyed the older bases of established authority in the West and is doing so throughout the world, although democracy itself will not in fact be achieved in most of the world in the near future. The rapid progress of communications intensifies every phase of these revolutions and indeed deserves itself separate characterization as the communications revolution. It involves such diverse elements as high speed diffusion of news and high speed travel, mass media, and in America, mass higher education. The culture contact between Western and non-Western cultures together with a vast amount of historical, critical, and social science research, reinforces and compounds the elements of relativism inherent in this modern Western experience.

Two facts stand out in attempting to assess the importance of these revolutionary processes. First of all, it now seems realistic to hope that with reason and good will poverty can be overcome and freedom won to provide the basis of truly humane living. There are formidable obstacles in the way of such an accomplishment, but the scientific transformations of our time give promise of the means. The human problems, however, which stand in the way are of tremendous magnitude. Second, the older view of man, what he is doing on the earth, what he ought to aim at, aspire to and bend his efforts to accomplish, is codified, often in contradictory terms, in the traditions of the past. Today this older view is seen as it stands to be quite insufficient to provide sure guides in this time of transition. The depth and the scope of this inadequacy in the face of great threat and great opportunity comprise the significant dimensions of the present crisis.

To face this situation requires that we eschew all forms of defensiveness in the face of the challenge and openly face the openness of our situation. It demands that we seriously attempt to understand our experience and our traditions, that we engage in a vast endeavor to clarify our experience and to interpret its implications with respect to our present condition. It is this effort at interpretation and clarification that must become central to the educational enterprise and to the religious life as well. In this book a series of essays is presented which attempt to examine some aspects, some dimensions, and some implications of this crisis. They attempt to cut beneath the shibboleths and superficialities of much discussion in both university and church circles, how successfully only continued discussion and effort will tell.

In the first chapter the crisis is treated as a crisis of the religious consciousness of our time seen in its typical range and variety against the background of what we have called the perennial crisis inherent in the religious experience and religious institutions. The second chapter takes us into the political sphere, for politics and religion have long been two areas in which men have found those experiences which express their deepest aspirations and made those interpretations which have significantly shaped their self-images and definitions of their situations. In this examination we attempt to understand the political dimensions of our contemporary situation as a background for making ourselves and making our history here and now in ways appropriate to our condition and our capacity. Having examined religion and politics we then turn to an examination of the three great strands of the Western spiritual and intellectual traditions—to religion, humanism and science. These three, always interrelated in the most intimate way, often in serious antagonism, constitute the formulated precipitate of the experience of Western man in dealing with himself, his work, his environment and his relationship to being.

It is argued in the third chapter that important though each of these undoubtedly is, they fail to provide basic guidance to Western man. Indeed Western man has evolved beyond the partial universes of each of them and faces the challenge of creating a newer and more adequate definition of the human condition. It must be a definition which utilizes the insights of all three while avoiding the blind spots and askewed vision of each. It must be an open and developing consciousness and not a hardened and crystalized ideology. And finally it must represent the many levels and aspects characteristic of man and his conditions with an ever growing adequacy. We cannot define human nature as something fixed and finally understood, but we must become aware of the extent of our knowledge of man and his situation as a background for the reasonable, dynamic and open-ended faith of the future. Next we look at the problems of contemporary youth. It is here that we see in sharpest outline the surfacing of the consciousness of crisis.

Many of our young people respond to today's world by making the Great Refusal. They see the institutions of their society as meaningless or even as corrupt and radically immoral. There is much worthy of serious attention in their judgment. But they stand intellectually paralyzed before the spectacle confronting them, unable to formulate positive programs or project positive aspirations with any realistic definition at all. Finally, we look at the problem of man making himself in our day. In this crisis we must not only take responsibility for remaking our culture and society, understanding that it will effect a transformation of ourselves. We must also come to understand how we can rationally and with comprehension guide and influence our own development. Never before has the conception of responsibility carried such a weighty and significant burden.

Implicit in this discussion is what used to be designated by believer and unbeliever alike as atheism. This word now takes on such ambiguity that its usefulness soon may become simply to point to the difficulty faced by modern man in attempting to discuss ultimates. Yet that very ambiguity points toward an increasingly profound grasp of what is involved in man's religious relationship, and the closely related problems involved in the language used to communicate older insights and interpret older experiences. Over half a century ago Leon Bloy distinguished the "atheists who believe in God" from the "atheists who do not believe in God," and the believers "who believe in God" from the believers "who do not believe in God." Such distinctions have become both more and less meaningful in our day. They stand less within the older tradition and the conflicts of the tradition, and point more to the necessities of new formulation. But such reformulation is a long-term historical process which will culminate from and reflect the experience of our time, clarified and interpreted in the light of our conflicting traditions, by a long process of study and dialogue. Such a process involves great scholarly and intellectual effort.

As is said in the second chapter of this book, "Man is emerging into the historical epoch in which the long implicit question 'what is man doing on this earth?' becomes a matter for conscious thought and genuine decision, a matter of practical policy—indeed perhaps a prerequisite for survival." Men must discover how to construct and develop new dynamic equivalents for the "community-tradition-authority" context now rendered obsolete by current developments. Such a gradual creation will demand immense efforts for clarification and meaningful interpretation of the modern experience. The present work is put forth as a modest contribution to this great clarification process.

I wish to thank the following for permitting me to use here material which had either first appeared in their pages, or which had been developed as lectures under their auspices:

Daedalus for "The Crisis of the Contemporary Religious Consciousness"; the Center for the Study of Democratic Institutions for "Politics and the Religious Crisis" and "Christianity, Humanism and Science"; the Joint Commission on Education and Cultivation of the Methodist Board of Missions for "Christianity and the Atheism of Contemporary Youth"; the Church Society for College

14   Alienation, Atheism and the Religious Crisis

Work for "Youth and the Search for Meaning," and the Harvard Divinity School for "The Real Challenge of Secularism." To each, I am deeply grateful.

Thomas F. O'Dea
Institute of Religious Studies
University of California at
Santa Barbara

1

The Crisis of the Contemporary Religious Consciousness

During times of religious crises, existence tends to be experienced in terms of its manifold contradictions. People have neither the noetic capacity to integrate an organized outlook nor the psychological ability to achieve a sense of meaningful participation in their society. In recent decades, this condition has come to characterize the outlook of strategic strata in Western countries. It represents a severe crisis of Western religious consciousness. There is much in the present situation that is not new; unbelief, ambivalence, and the temptation of nihilism have characterized religious crises in the past. The inherently close but fundamentally incompatible relationship between faith and doubt is a permanent and perennial characteristic of the religious experience. Yet the conditions of Western man today present this perennial and abiding element of crisis in a new setting—a dynamic and secularized society embodying a scientific world view.

This new setting alters radically both the meaning of the perennial crisis and the modes of handling it available to men. At the same time, the combination of perennial and novel elements creates a genuinely new human situation and justifies speaking in terms of the crisis of contemporary religious consciousness. Still, this crisis is experienced differently by people from different social backgrounds, cultural traditions, and religious faiths. But whatever be the differential incidence and different degrees of involvement in the crisis among the various groups in America and the West, the democratization of higher education brings the crisis and involvement in it to ever increasing numbers.

For a sociologist to attempt an analysis of this crisis is to undertake a task that transcends the conceptual tools of his profession, however useful they may prove in certain respects. Behind any analysis of this kind lies an individual experience, a particular perspective, a personal vision. The overview of any writer on this topic will reflect both his professional and his personal biography, his own individual confrontation of and mode of adjustment to the basic elements of the crisis. In the present case, it reflects not only two decades spent in the scholarly study of man's historical and social existence, particularly in relation to his cultural productions and his religious concerns, but also a life lived in a time of war and revolution, of chaotic violence and routinized extermination, of rising expectations and increasing anxieties, of promise and unprecedented threat to man's future.

Intellectual and sociological analysis alone can delineate the elements of crisis; this will be attempted with soberness and objectivity. But the configuration they assume will reveal the significance that the analyst sees in them or attributes to them, a significance that expresses not only objective reality but the author's relation to the world. What is attempted here will be a reasonable and open-minded exposition of one sociologist's view of the con-

temporary religious crisis, eschewing both the smug flat-
tening out of disturbing implications that some social
scientists mistake for objectivity and the overdramatic
wallowing in catastrophe of certain of their intellectual
critics.

Four aspects of the contemporary religious crisis, each
of which deserves more attention than can be given it
within the scope of this article, will be investigated: (1)
the range and variety of crisis experiences; (2) the perennial elements of the religious crisis; (3) the urgency of the
contemporary situation; (4) the available modes for confronting the crisis. These aspects will be sketched here,
but will re-appear as themes throughout the book.

THE RANGE AND VARIETY OF CRISIS EXPERIENCES

Let us begin by describing in ideal typical, and somewhat
foreshortened and stereotyped terms several kinds of
people recognizably suffering in one way or another from
the implications of the religious crisis.

We start with a bright Italian-American student on the
campus of a Catholic college. Reared in a traditional
Catholic home, he attended a parochial elementary and
high school and is now in his junior year of college. He
is a major in the humanities or the social sciences and has
read widely, especially in serious modern thought and
literature. He strongly identifies with Catholic intellectuals critical of the tenor of American Catholic life, with
progressive theologians, and with the so-called "liberal"
party at Vatican II. He champions ecumenism and litur-
gical revival within his church and is generally sympathetic
to new departures in religious thought and action. He
considers the problem for people like himself to be that

of developing a contemporary and relevant Catholicism that remains, at the same time, true to itself as the bearer of an authentic hierophany. He sees the religion of his parents and, even more, that of his grandparents as "folk" Catholicism, once a protective cocoon for a living religious tradition and experience but now thoroughly dysfunctional for people like himself. He thinks that his fellow students who take refuge in conservative politics or in a combination of conservative politics with a preconciliar Catholicism are practicing an ostrich-like obscurantism, forgivable in aging priests but lamentable, if not reprehensible, in his contemporaries. To him, many of his older clerical teachers and pastors, and possibly his bishop, vary from well-meaning but ineffectual religious conservatives to religious neanderthalers. Beneath this posture—as genuine and authentic as possible for him—there lurk both anguish and dread. He experiences genuine crises of meaning and the real threat of meaninglessness.

We leave the Catholic college and go to a nearby secular campus. Here we see a young man, Jewish by descent, who was brought up in a socially mobile family in which religious teaching, religious atmosphere, or religious concern was at a minimum. He has taken courses in history and the social sciences. In college he has discovered that he is a Jew, not in the sense that he had somehow always known it, but in a new way. He has discovered that there exists a religious, an intellectual, and a legal tradition in which the term *Jew* takes on new meaning for him. He puts on a yarmulke, perhaps even begins to grow a beard, learns Hebrew—or rediscovers the value of some he reluctantly learned in childhood—becomes meticulous concerning dietary regulations and the proper observance of the Sabbath. His secular friends, also of Jewish background, ridicule him somewhat good-naturedly for his "Jew-cap" and his interest in "pilpul," but they nevertheless sense something significant in his behavior. Moreover, they feel that his behavior relates them to him through some unvoiced bond. He is not always sure what he believes about the God of Abraham, Isaac, and Jacob, but his mentors assure him that with faithful observance in terms of what have been called "action symbols" the rest will somehow take care of itself. Beneath this posture— as genuine and authentic as possible for him—there lurk uncertainty and nervousness, which sometimes issue in inner desperation, sometimes in outer aggressiveness.

In a nearby school of theology we observe a young American Protestant from a small town in the Middle West. He is a candidate for the degree of Bachelor of Divinity. Although he studies the traditional subjects prescribed for such a course, he is intensely interested in protest movements, especially those which he thinks involve an ethical challenge. He is aware of the current theological situation in American Protestantism, and he is confused by it. The "obsolescence" of the Social Gospel, the "contributions" of neo-orthodoxy, the "challenge" of the Death-of-God theology affect him, but often leave him groping for a sense of direction. He is not sure what he believes, but he has maintained the notion that through the Christian idiom in some way, and within the context of the churches somehow, he can and will find the path to the experience that will relate him significantly to life. He participates in protests against the war in Vietnam and joins the marches for civil rights. In these activities he may meet the two young men sketched above; if he does, he will experience a momentary but exhilarating epiphany of ecumenicity and solidarity. Through it all he looks for a more profound epiphany—a showing forth of the divine for which he still uses the sacred name of Christ. He is not certain he believes in God or what belief in God really means; nor is he clear about what Christ means to him. Still, he hopes for the authenticity of his goal and is convinced of the genuineness of his search. Beneath this posture—as genuine and authentic as possible for him—lurk self-diffusion and anxiety, which at times throw him into fits of depression and at others provide him with the energy for heroic action.

There are many other types of young people seeking significance in action, in politics, in psychedelic drugs, in sexual experimentation. All of them are touched in some way by the contemporary crisis that has so deeply affected the relevance and significance of traditional and institutionalized religion today. But let us look for a moment at the older generation.

In a sizable city in a southwestern state there is a banker—head of a medium-sized commercial bank—who belongs to a family long prominent in the region. The population has grown greatly in the last two decades, and his position in the community has become less visible, less secure. Moreover, in the nation as a whole, changes in corporate business, in the tax structure, and in the role of government in economic life have created a new world in which he does not feel at home. Politics have changed, and the international situation reveals a world in which he feels strange and more than a little afraid. Changes in the relationship of the races have instituted a world he never made, one that he finds difficult to understand. His daughter returns from college—and not an eastern college either—with ideas on all these topics and even on the relationships of the sexes that bring home to him the frightening quality of his newly recognized status as stranger, as outsider. He is sure of one thing, one stable element in his life—his membership in the United Presbyterian Church. He has been its constant supporter, although irregular in attendance. His Presbyterianism has always been part of his selfhood, alongside his bankership, his Republicanism, and his family lineage. He has also been attracted to conservative politics, in which he has sought some defense—at least symbolic—of a better day.

One morning a couple of years ago, he picked up his morning paper to find that the Stated Clerk, the highest elected officer of his denomination, had been arrested on a civil rights picket line. The world he was holding together so precariously threatened then and there to come apart. Fortunately for him, he found a local schismatic Presbyterian church that combined fundamentalist religion with radical-right politics. He now finds his refuge in this group. With this man we can speak less of a posture than of a condition, but it is a condition that draws near to the edge of the void that can threaten human consciousness when one is out of step with a world one cannot understand.

In an eastern city there is a Roman Catholic pastor who has served a local church for thirty years, first as curate and then as parish priest. He is an Irish-American. Graduating from the diocesan seminary of his day, he learned little sophisticated theology and soon after ordination found himself so involved in the practical tasks of his pastoral assignment that he had little time for theology at all. Throughout the years he found his parish to be a bastion of traditional belief surrounded by what seemed like a sea of indifference, unbelief, and even aggressively anti-religious sentiment. He lived through the local repercussions of the Spanish Civil War. He and his parishioners saw that war as the struggle of the forces of unbelief against a Catholic nation and culture. His non-Catholic neighbors who had other associations with Spanish history than those of the Irish-Catholic memory saw different values at stake in the Iberian struggle. He experienced the 1930's as an increasingly "red decade" and during the forties saw his country an ally of militantly atheistic and anti-religious Soviet Russia. He was aware of the reality of danger to his faith and to the world in which his own variety of that faith had been at home. In the early 1950's he rejoiced temporarily in the exorcism of the threat by the late Senator Joseph McCarthy. The calm of the late fifties under a conservative president was a relief to him. He received some ambivalent satisfaction in 1960 with the election of a member of his church to the highest office in the land and the end of the last shred of the stigma of his second-class citizenship, but he was quite aware that the outlook of the new President was perilously close to the secular liberalism that had threatened him all his life.

Then came Vatican II, which reversed the basic religious tone in which he had been reared and which had been reinforced in his adult experience on almost every crucial issue. It looked to him as though the Catholic Church was indeed being protestantized. He continued to obey his superiors, grateful when they put the brakes on this *aggiornamento,* as they frequently did. He is really not sure what to make of it all. Questions from his parishioners—a new phenomenon in his parish—irritate him, especially those on birth control. He fears the apostasy of the young. He still believes—believes in the Nicene Creed, believes that he offers Christ to the Father in his morning

Mass. But it becomes harder and harder to relate these beliefs to the world about him—even to the church about him. Sometimes, like T.S. Eliot's magus, he "would be glad of another death." To him the world seems to be approaching chaos—what the ancient Hindu writers called the "confusion of castes." He, also, seeks some succor in right-wing politics, but his troubles are deeper, and his surcease must be sought elsewhere. He manages to maintain the traditional posture, but within he is a baffled and defeated man.

This list could be prolonged with profit. We could consider the Mormon youth who, uneasy in the religion of his forebears, is searching for a new stance by rebelling against the symbols of the older provincial orthodoxy or by embracing them with an over-determined rigidity and a heightened defensiveness. Or the southern youth at the northern university who embraces a new liberalism in hopes of finding both an outlet for the moral conviction imbibed from a Christianity in which he can no longer believe and a way of entering and participating in the larger, unprovincial, intellectual world. Yet for him, beneath this genuine and useful posture, lurk real guilt for his revolt against his fathers and his deviance from regional loyalties, and resentment of any condescension involved in his acceptance by his new northern friends. We might also consider those young people who seek meaning in new secular ideologies that offer themselves as the psychological, functional equivalents of religion. Or we might continue to examine the older and more established who seek in professional identifications and activities sufficient self-definition and expression to keep the inroads of the current crisis at a distance.

All of these represent people who are trying to live in

and cope with change—change in society, change in thinking and styles of life, change in education, in community structure, in the churches. The younger ones are looking for a self-definition with which to face life; the older ones are clinging to an old identity rooted in circumstances and beliefs, habits and values now being rendered irrelevant. Other elements beside the religious crisis are involved in these personal predicaments. Personal crises are always to be found in times of social change; but in this time of exceptionally rapid social change they are more numerous and more significant. Moreover, beneath the contemporary identity crises hides the void created beneath the institutionalized assumptions by the religious crisis itself. These little stereotyped biographies, those described and those suggested, are idiosyncratic and selective refractions of the spiritual history of today. They are as real a part of the present crisis as the explicit anxieties of the intellectuals who attempt to formulate and meet the problems involved on the explicit conceptual level.

These representative biographical types—representative, of course, in the Emersonian rather than the statistical sense—not only mirror the spiritual condition of our time; they also reflect the history of America. Immigration and assimilation, westward expansion, industrialization and urbanization, the communications revolution, and the increasing democratization of education on all levels have all affected the American milieu. Each American religion seems at present to occupy its own half-way house in which defense of its traditions and its vested interests is found in short-term adjustment to a severe situation for which no final solutions are envisaged. The biographies of all Americans reflect the profound uneasiness of the religious communities.

Moreover, the different religious traditions place different emphases upon the role of ideas in religious life. Consequently intellectual issues affect some groups more directly than they do others. Because Catholicism continues the patristic and medieval synthesis of religion and culture and emphasizes the central significance of intellectual assent in the act of faith, it is most vulnerable to the pressures of intellectual scepticism and conflicting ideologies. Protestantism, though deeply affected by the challenge of intellectual research, study, and theorizing in philosophy and Bible study, has faced modernity with less defensiveness, though hardly with fewer debilitating consequences. Moreover, the residual effects of Protestantism's earlier unofficial establishment in America has made it, on the whole, far less defensive before the challenges of modern life. In American Judaism, the substrate of ethnic identity and the abiding centrality of the family have enabled many to accept any ideological, philosophical, or religious position and to remain in some sense Jews. Thus, within these three traditions, the identity crisis and the religious crisis are likely to be differently related and to assume different forms. For those of secularist background—an old and honored tradition in the history of America—the progressive impetus of traditional conceptions appears to share in the general crisis and to offer little to the oncoming generation in its search for identity and meaning.

THE RELIGIOUS CRISIS: ITS PERENNIAL ELEMENTS

The primal crisis of religious consciousness is revealed, albeit covertly, in religious myth, the earliest and most holistic form of religious expression. Myth, to use the terminology of Theodor Gaster, translates reality into ideal terms and preserves the momentary experience by giving it duration. Myth, moreover, is the affirmation by man that he is at home in his world—that he belongs, a being among the many beings, in the orderly and meaningful world of his experience. Yet myth is the obvious product of consciousness and imagination—the creation of a being who has already eaten of the Tree of Knowledge and has, thereby, disrupted a psychic, primal harmony with reflection, questioning, and doubt. Myth reveals itself to the modern scholar as a meaningful assertion made in the face of a potential threat of meaninglessness. It can be inferred, in a manner analogous to that by which Freud posited the existence of unconscious motivation, that there existed for mythic man a potential crisis of consciousness; this became the setting for myth-creation and for an assertion, through myth and ritual, of "faith" in a world of meaning. In the face of possible doubt, myth declares man's relationship to and significance in the world of his experience.

But man not only related himself to the world of his experience; he also attempted to exert control over elements of his surroundings. According to L. S. B. Leakey, some two million years ago *Homo habilis* made and made use of tools. As man slowly extended his control over nature, he increased and multiplied and according to the modest standards of his time proceeded to subdue the earth. Alongside this growing mastery and intricately related to its later stages, mythic apprehension and expression made way for logical conceptualization and rational discourse. Men broke through the enchanted garden of the mythic world.

Earlier man had made a peculiar kind of relation to

his total situation: He apprehended it and responded to it as "sacred" through ritual and myth. Man's success in developing his control over nature and his consequent development of new forms of social existence introduced and enlarged areas of experience from which the sacred quality was removed. In thought, as in action, manipulation produced a world more and more shorn of its emotional and projective character. The fruits of these developments are to be seen in the agriculture and engineering, the administrative and legal structures of the ancient empires, and the growing sophistication technologically and strategically of the conduct of war. They assume a new quality, however, in the peculiar religious experience of the Hebrews. By positing the existence of a transcendent God, the Hebrews demythologized the earth, thereby emancipating man from the magic circle of older religious world-views. Whatever may seem the mythological character of the Bible to modern man, biblical religion stands in stark contrast with myth in its genuine form. Moreover, the rationalizing implications of men's thought and effort reached their manifest expression in Greek philosophy. Socrates showed men how to overcome myth, demonstrating that they could achieve a new freedom through the positive power of self-knowledge. His contribution was joined to those of the Hebrew Bible by the Fathers of the Christian church. In a great creative adjustment, they brought into being the religious core of the cultural epoch of European civilization.

Yet biblical religion and Hellenic rationality could not do away with the primal crisis involving the simultaneity and incompatibility of faith and doubt that lay at the core of religion in its mythic form. Three instances sufficiently demonstrate the way in which this basic crisis comes to the surface of man's consciousness in the Hebrew and Hellenic contexts. Within the Hebrew Bible is an odd book whose inclusion in the canon has long perplexed the pious and puzzled the scholarly. The ruminations of Qoheleth—known as Ecclesiastes, the Greek transformation of his name—present an example of religious crisis. They show that the emancipation from myth together with its positive religious achievements uncovered and revealed more fully the crisis elements primordially lurking at the core of man's religious experience. Uprooted from the closed community of his forebears, Qoheleth lived in the wider world that trade and war had created. Under the conditions of Jewish life in the early Hellenistic period, he spoke to men as individuals facing intimately the problem of meaning.

Qoheleth's religion reflects his confrontation of the threat of meaninglessness and cosmic aloneness that lay concealed behind the mythic assertion of earlier religions and the belief and hope in a relation to a transcendent God of his Hebrew forefathers. He sees a world characterized by movement without genuine change, effort without authentic profit. Events are predetermined, but their reasonable comprehension remains forever impossible. All values are negated by their opposites, just as life eventually is by death. The facts of life contradict the optimistic Hebraic idea that retribution from God inevitably overtakes evil and that goodness is repaid in prosperity. Neither character nor works affect one's fate. Before the incomprehensible frustrations and enigmas of human life, Qoheleth cries, "A vapor of vapors! All is vapor!" But he does not despair completely. Rather, he seeks to find happiness in a kind of anemic vitalism by enjoying the day-to-day experience of living itself and avoiding the restlessness and unhappiness inevitably involved in straining after religious peace and certitude. What Qoheleth sees and recommends to others is the little life of modest ambitions in a disenchanted world.

The mythic assertion concerns itself with the problem of meaning, to which the problem of evil is central. Biblical religion attempts to handle the problem of evil even more optimistically than had many older mythic views. "Right will protect the blameless life, but sin overturns the wicked" (Prov. XII:6). Qoheleth's disenchantment challenges this view, but it is questioned most seriously and most poignantly in the Book of Job. In this great inconclusive classic of theodicy, a righteous man is overwhelmed by disaster and subjected to the taunts of his conventionally righteous associates. The Book of Job fails to answer the question of how the facts of existence can be reconciled with the reality of divine justice or the existence of a benevolent Providence. Job expresses faith as his solution. Although based upon despair and resignation, his is a faith nevertheless capable of asserting unshakable trust and genuine hope. Through Job's suffering there is brought into existence the religion of the "twice born." Unlike Qoheleth's mild, this-wordly resignation and his acceptance of a naïve natural enjoyment of life, Job finds the stance of faith as the mode of conquering meaninglessness and aloneness.

Nihilism remains a constant potential of religious thought and feeling. With the broadening of human experience and the rationalization of thought, nihilism threatens increasingly to come to the surface. Its most impressive surfacing may be seen at the beginning of the Christian era in the religion of the Gnostics.

The Gnostics, various as they were, saw a world from

which men were fundamentally estranged, a world produced by an evil or, at best, a neutral and inferior creator. Men must find emancipation from this world through esoteric knowledge of a hidden god and his ways. Man's was not a disharmony of body and soul because of sin, but an ontological dualism rendering him an acosmic being, radically alien in and alienated from the world. Gnosticism represents a desperate faith driven to find an answer to its severe disarticulation with existence in an escape to a god who is himself alien to the world of human experience in the most fundamental way.

Doubt was not unfamiliar to Jeremiah and the Prophets, nor to deeply religious men of all ages who plumbed the depths and discovered the religious crisis for themselves. But doubt was confronted and resolved by incorporating it into a larger affirmation of faith. God may chastise men, he may even appear to desert them, but he was ultimately just; God was God.

The Christian church accepted the conviction of classical antiquity from Plato to the Stoics that the world was a *cosmos,* a knowable order, and that there existed a fundamental harmony between this order and man's nature. It brought together this conviction with its Hebraic antecedents. God was thought to reveal to mankind knowledge of himself and of the path to salvation. The harmony of microcosm and macrocosm transcended the world; man's ultimate place was determined by his eternal relationship to God. Peter Lombard (1100/1164?) in his *Four Books of Sentences,* which from the thirteenth to the sixteenth century was the most important single work in European religious education, said that man can achieve knowledge of the invisible things of God "through creatures visible and invisible. For he was aided by two means, namely by nature which was rational and by works performed by God that truth might be manifested to man." Christianity succeeded in burying for centuries the possibilities of radical nihilism to which Gnostic religion had given expression. But doubt came to plague Christianity, as its late medieval resort to inquisitorial and authoritarian repression sadly testifies. The elements of crisis continued to lurk beneath the surface throughout the ages of faith themselves.

First to be doubted was the second of Peter Lombard's propositions—that God had performed works that truth might be made manifest to man. The first proposition— that nature was rational and that rational man was, therefore, at home in the world—stood up longer. Religious doubt in early modern times did not, by and large, transgress the cosmological and human limits of earlier Christian views. Progress replaced Providence; perfectibility through grace gave way to perfectibility through effort. The city of man belonged in the world of nature. History was no longer a religious drama but a natural process.

But pessimism—and behind it the threat of meaninglessness, of spiritual nothingness—continued to lurk beneath the surface of an optimistic revolt against otherwordly religion. Even Descartes, who saw in science the instrument to make man the "master and possessor of nature," and who dared to turn doubt into a method, toyed with the Gnostic hypothesis that an evil genius might have created the world. By joining subjective and objective in an ontological argument for God's existence, he found his personal and intellectual solution and, concomitantly, the necessary basis for his world-view. In Hume's philosophy, secularized optimism was itself seriously challenged. Human reason was not self-sufficient, but rested upon premises beyond proof. Kant answered Hume, but in a way that undermined once and for all a comfortable acceptance of such premises as self-evident. Earlier, Pascal had faced, as a Christian, the implications of man's aloneness in the new world that science and philosophy were making known. He saw a silent universe that did not answer man's cry or longing, but remained alien and indifferent to his aspirations. Before the incomprehensible immensity of that world Pascal was frightened. He came to see man's aspirations rooted in reasons beyond reason and made his wager on a hidden God who was still the God of Christianity. Yet he retained the classic pride in man's capacities—a thinking reed superior thereby to a universe that might at any moment crush him.

Science has revealed to man a world with which he has no inner resonance; it has trained him to a stance toward the world which makes lack of mystic response "natural," "proper," and "objective." Moreover, the scientific study of man himself has revealed a historical and ontological relativity concerning all human accomplishments and productions—whether in thought or in life. Cultures and societies stand revealed as "compromise formations" formed from competing interests, points of view, and cognitive perspectives upon the world of experience. Entities of limited durability, they are destined to pass away. Indeed, individual identity itself is seen to be problematic, highly dependent upon circumstances; most cherished spiritual achievements rest upon a potential void. Social science has rediscovered in a new idiom the older mythic insight into the relation of primal order to primal chaos. But is modern man able to make an act of faith and an assertion of resonance comparable with that made in myth and in Jewish and Christian religion?

While these developments characterized the emerging modern consciousness, Christianity tended to become either a culture religion raising no fundamentally disturbing questions or to remain in a spiritual ghetto in militant opposition to developing modernity. Kierkegaard experienced this alienation, this estrangement from the world of being; he sought escape in an act of faith more desperate than the wager of Pascal. Nietzsche saw nihilism, "this weirdest of all guests," standing before the door of his century and the world standing before man as a "gate to deserts stretching mute and chill." Projecting himself in his parable of the madman, he proclaimed, "God is dead. God remains dead. And we have killed him."

Modern developments bring the perennial latent crisis to actuality and in a setting shorn of traditional compensations. Modern men appear to make two fundamental responses within the general tradition. Following Job (and Pascal and Kierkegaard), they attempt to posit an act of faith; or like Qoheleth, they seek in mundane experience—not just daily trivia but this-wordly experience seen in the this-worldly frame of reference of the Enlightenment, often seasoned with Christian elements—satisfactions of an ante-penultimate character. Thus is revealed the neo-Christianity and the neo-Stoicism of today. Both accept the deeper substrate—the reasons beyond reason of Pascal—in one form or another. Man has aspirations, he displays an effort after the ethical, but he is not part of a cosmos with whose immanent logos he can feel any sustained and dependable kinship. He is a stranger creating meaning out of his own estrangement. His reflective acts reveal his naked aloneness in a nature that is purposeless. He clings to values that lack all ontological support.

Existence is seen by some as absurd; man, once the cap-stone of creation, is but a futile passion. Men struggle with their absurdity and, in accepting it, attempt to transcend it.

The cosmic backdrop of medieval Christianity or of Enlightenment unbelief has dropped away and with it the resonance between subjective orientation and objective setting upon which all cultures have ultimately rested. The lurking primal crisis of the religious consciousness is unveiled for modern man. He may either accept it with faith or with stoic resignation, or attempt to avoid it in the busyness of less than ultimate pursuits. Writing in the 19th century, John Henry Newman told how Napoleon responded to his excommunication by asking, "Does the Pope think that the muskets will fall from the hands of my soldiers?" Newman commented that a few years later the muskets literally did fall from the hands of the Emperor's troops on the plains of Russia. Men who consider themselves in some sense "religious" have smiled at this story. Yet how many modern men could make such a statement as Newman's in today's world? This was the point of view of the prophets, of the evangelists, of the Fathers, of the Reformers. Its practical disappearance marks the end of an epoch and heralds a form of the religious crisis unique in the history of Western man. Nietzsche's guest stands in our midst.

THE RELIGIOUS CRISIS: ITS CONTEMPORARY
URGENCY

Genuine religious experience issuing in authentic faith and wholeness of spirit and combining with contemporary relevance has become increasingly rare and difficult. Consequently this age lacks relevant religious exemplars. Today, as in past ages, most men adhere to religions by a more or less uncritical acceptance of what is established. But conventional religion has always depended ultimately upon the existence of the profound and authentic religious experience of its *megalopsychoi*—the great souled ones. Without that, even conventional religion falters. It draws its strength from the past, which it does little to preserve at the deeper psychological level. In this situation institutional religion displays two kinds of irrelevance. Either it has maintained some significant personal meaning for its adherents, but has lost a relationship to man's larger history; or it struggles to attain historical relevance and exhibits little personal significance for ordinary men. Seen in itself this represents a severe and advanced form of religious crisis, but when viewed in the total setting of modern man a new urgency and even desperation is brought to light.

Men have achieved the technical capacity to alter the conditions of human life to an extent that was undreamed of even twenty years ago, but these very men in the advanced industrial countries are unable to go beyond piecemeal and contradictory programs in shaping these conditions. Ivan Karamazov commented that without God everything is possible. Modern man has experienced to his sorrow what this can mean. But it is also true that without God nothing is possible; man can now also experience what this means. In the development of technology a great bureaucratic structure has been elaborated. All men, except the "culturally deprived," fit into this structure; they have become parts of a great social machine. The social relationships and institutions formed to enable men to control the world of nature have become a second nature controlling them.

Modern man finds himself consuming in order to work, reversing the ancient casual formula; in a hundred ways he adapts himself to the social leviathan he has brought into being. Mastery over nature has become objectified into a social structure that controls all men. The capacities of technology for humanizing life have not been realized. As the irrationality of such a situation becomes more evident, the possibility of a rational understanding of the human situation and of programs based upon this understanding recedes beyond the grasp of the immense intellectual establishment. In fact this establishment has become increasingly integrated into the great machine as the provider of the trained personnel which it more and more requires. Among the peoples of the world not simply discord but potential chaos threatens continually. In the West the problem-solving mentality, the product of science and pragmatic effort, finds itself capable of solving any problem, but without the reservoir of world-view and value-orientation that would define and attribute priority to needs and aspirations of contemporary men. The problem-solving mentality reigns supreme, but it does not rule. Rather, it adapts itself to the initiative of circumstances and the caprice of events. The use of reason in the broad service of life retreats before the mind of modern man to join the powers and principalities of myth and the God of the Bible. Without an orientation to being, modern man cannot put himself together into a whole. Having lost transcendence, he finds himself without practical leverage in effectively changing his world. Without God or his memory in Enlightenment philosophy, he no longer knows what it means to be man and hence cannot utilize his enormous capacities to humanize the conditions of his life.

The irrational, affluent societies of the advanced industrial countries begin more and more to resemble the society projected in the imagination of Auguste Comte—a technocracy dominated by the organizers of industry and knowledge. Today, however, the military must be added. In the present Comtean condition, the three religious traditions play the role of the "religion of humanity," often shedding even their partial and truncated transcendence for a common "civic religion." In a world that cries out for authentic transcendence and genuine community, the trumpets of conventional religiosity give forth the sounds of uncertainty. Enlightenment philosophers naïvely hoped that by crushing the "infamy" of supernatural religion and liberating men from the tyranny of a supernatural city of God, men would be free to construct a humane, this-wordly city of man. These hopes threaten to become as remote as Jeremiah's and Newman's Yahwistic notions of a divine and providential lord of history. In this situation certain people, the more stubborn, the more sensitive, or the more disturbed, attempt to assert a measure of freedom and transcendence in sheer refusal—combating the absurd with the absurd. Their efforts, confused and confusing, assume a bewildering variety of forms.

Since the establishment of Charlemagne's Empire, Christianity has provided the noetic integrator and the spiritual sustenance that made possible the rise of Europe as a sociological and historical reality. It provided convictions in terms of which man could act and judge action, develop discourse, and project self-realization. Today man lives on the echoes and memories of that situation. In the face of current opportunity and contemporary urgency, most people are unable to believe with the depth and fervor that would provide direction to their thinking and motivation for their actions in meeting the demands of modernity. Nor are they able to disbelieve with the genuineness, conviction, and vigor that would produce the creative negation that might eventuate in a new and positive human orientation. In the past the recalcitrance of nature, human and nonhuman, separated ideal and real. Today, inability to form the ideal with reason and conviction leaves man controlled by circumstances, despite the enormous capacities of his technological rationality.

MODES OF ADJUSTMENT TO THE RELIGIOUS CRISIS

Some men avoid the contemporary religious crisis by relying upon an enlightened and sophisticated common sense. Accepting older values as humanly self-evident although without ontological foundation, they leave questioning to those whom they consider esoteric and impractical. Scientific research, human understanding, human rights, abolition of hunger, the "Great Society" are all ideals derived from the older situation. Although they still seem adequate, it is sometimes noticed that these old war cries no longer stir the troops, especially the young recruits, as they once did. Other men stay within the safe confines of academic disciplines and professional pursuits. They do not question fundamentally the implications of their methodology, their results, or their functions. Within particular institutions petty authoritarianism may be practiced to keep out dangerous thoughts likely to infect the young and untried. Such behavior is by no means peculiar to religious institutions. The resulting fragmentation of intellectual and spiritual life passively abets the developing crisis situation.

How, in fact, is the crisis to be met? Concern for the religious quality of contemporary life or belated urges to return to the classics in education appear almost the gestures of a bored and defeated complacency. Obviously, spirituality today needs its authentically relevant exemplars, and reason its humanly relevant embodiment. The history of religious crises suggests certain solutions.

It would be possible to institutionalize religion in the old way with some functional equivalent of a church presiding over society, yet reasonably accommodated to its needs. Here the model in history is the medieval church; in philosophy, Plato's *Republic* and *Laws*. New generations would be brought up within a culturally sanctioned "right reason"; a genuine, if strait-jacketed, transcendence would offer satisfaction to men's religious needs. Yet the church discovered it needed inquisitions, and Plato foresaw the need of a night council. This solution did not prove viable in more appropriate historical conditions; it had to break up or eventuate in tyranny. Post-Tridentine Catholicism attempted to institutionalize a version of this solution within its own ranks. That, too, proved of ambiguous value and has been abandoned by Vatican II. The solution of such an institutionalization of religion is virtually closed for it would entail serious spiritual regression.

The present situation of pluralism of religions in a secular society could be prolonged and primacy given to secular values. While superior to the first solution, this half-way house offers no final escape from the current predicament. The present religious communions continue to transmit the spiritual heritage with varying degrees of profundity and success. The present religious dialogue continues to place before men the reality of the religious challenge. But the old heaven and the old earth have irretrievably passed away. The language of religion remains ambiguous and confusing. Sometimes it points the way to deeper spiritual realities; other times it beguiles its listeners with obsolescent memories.

Attention might be shifted from religious confrontation to the attempt to utilize the findings and methods of the social sciences in constructing secular communities and developing secure ego-formation among children. The conscious development of family life, friendship, and local community might attack the problem more successfully. Yet such a program requires value-consensus on both a small and a large scale. In quest of value-consensus, men would encounter all the problems of the current religious crisis head on. Matthew Arnold could appeal to love and urge men to be true to one another. A few years ago Archibald MacLeish could propose love as the final solution in his dramatic reworking of the Book of Job. But it appears a remnant of the Western religious tradition that by itself does not promise to generate either its own motivation or justification.

A possible solution could also be found in the new nationalisms. Yet the Communism of the Chinese, the nationalism of the Arabs, Africans, and Asians, the Zionism of Israel, and the sense of mission of America and France are also half-way houses of ambiguous value. While any rational philosophy will recognize the just demands of the secular community and its proper claims for individual support, it must provide for individual consciousness and effort. Nationalistic reasons beyond reason contain dangerous possibilities, as history has so unmistakably demonstrated.

The current attempt to find meaning in the ultimate admission of absurdity could provide still another solution. Here many follow the injunction of Joseph Conrad —in the destructive element, immerse—and seek significance in the sheer experiential quality of experience. The possibilities are great, ranging from the ascetic, crypto-Christian action-mysticism of T. E. Lawrence to the newer, less confined "holiness" of Saint Genet. In these terms, all escapes from the limited world of contemporary consciousness, all plunges into the unconscious are seen as possibly productive of spiritual worth. Sexual experience, available to the poorest of the underprivileged as Ernst Toller once observed, becomes a favorite area for experimentation, though by no means the exclusive one. New drugs promise new possibilities. Extreme experiences lived at a heightened intensity substitute for and replace the religious experience. It is difficult to see at present the ultimate significance of this important current development. It alone does not appear capable of effecting spiritual and cultural metamorphoses.

II

Politics
and the Religious Crisis

The political situation and the religious crisis are best understood as two aspects of a deeper crisis characteristic of the current condition of Western thought and culture. Politics and religion are both to be understood as kinds of human response or types of human activity which express man's deeper interests and aspirations. It is a serious mistake to see them as merely segmented portions of human thinking, feeling and action. They express deeper levels of man which come forward in political and religious activity and become objectified in intellectual, aesthetic and institutional forms. We do not understand very much about this human potential except by examination of how it has revealed itself under specific historical conditions in the past. The long struggle between Church and State since Gregory VII was a fight between two authority structures attempting to exert a strategic hegemony over the evolving European community. Each represented a different way of organizing the human community and a different model for the self-realization of the human potential. In America, the secular mode of organizing the community—indeed of organizing the holy community

of God's "almost chosen people," to use Lincoln's term—
came early to be the preferred mode, and American
religion adapted to it by the development of denomina-
tionalism, an historic development earlier seen as the form
of the future by John Locke.[1] The basic relationship
between religion and politics as two forms of expressing
man's potential was first clearly seen by Hegel.[2] The
human spirit objectified itself and advanced dialectically
in these two spheres of human thought and action.

The second preliminary point follows from the first.
Today we are in a religious crisis, and we are in a political crisis in something more than a surface understanding
of that word. They are both part of a deeper crisis of
consciousness in which Western man is becoming aware
of himself in a new way. Men have lived up to our epoch
largely determined in their aims, aspirations, actions and
accomplishments by their experience in specific historical
settings. Gradually they have achieved some degree of
mastery over conditions and some degree of self-determination with respect to them. But so far as we know, never
in the human experience has the possibility of human
beings taking conscious responsibility for self-realization
become a practical possibility as it is becoming today.
Writing in 1845, Karl Marx said: "The materialistic
doctrine that men are the products of conditions and
education, different men therefore the products of other
conditions and changed education, forgets that circumstances may be altered by men and that the educator has
himself to be educated."[3]

Today that point of leverage at which we can choose
our circumstances and thereby make ourselves, anticipated by Marx over a century ago, has arrived. Permit
me to repeat here what I have written elsewhere: "The fact

is that the two sides of the basic ecological relationship—men vis-a-vis situation—have been opened up. Man is no longer so highly conditioned by his circumstances since he has increased his control over circumstances tremendously and by his growing critical capacity and self-awareness has come to have some intellectual leverage over society, tradition and the conditioning process. The forms of institutions and custom no longer enjoy the kind of self-evident validation and untouchable status that they had in earlier societies. Man is emancipated to some considerable degree from both environment and tradition. He is in a position to choose his activity, his values, his self-development. Man is being increasingly placed in the situation in which he must choose what he will do, how he will employ his immense technical potential, his vast capacity to make his world; he is simultaneously being put in the circumstances in which he must make major decisions about what is of true worth in the human venture. Here he discovers that his emancipation has had another side. The overcoming of tradition has too often been the emptying out of substance. No way has been developed satisfactorily to bring forward the insights of the tradition in universal and communicable form and at the same time profit from the development of self-consciousness and the critical faculty.

In such circumstances men experience a most fundamental anomie and in confronting it often behave regressively and seek out old systems of belief and old postures which are unsuitable to the new conditions. What is more serious is that they often know at a deeper level, which they try to keep beneath the threshold of full awareness, that what they are doing is highly contrived. Emotional catharsis, an insecure identity, and stalemate result and substitute for more fruitful attempts to meet the issue. Man cannot avoid this situation which he has created. He must learn to face up to the challenge to make his world and to make himself—to realize himself according to a design which will do most justice to his potential. Man is emerging into the historical epoch in which the long implicit question "what is man doing on this earth?" becomes a matter for conscious thought and genuine decision, a matter of practical policy—indeed perhaps a prerequisite for survival."[4] Marx's famous final thesis on Feuerbach takes on a remarkable practicality in our day. "Philosophers have only interpreted the world differently, but the point is to change it."[5]

A few further remarks about this two-fold crisis are in order. To the extent that we suffer the severe disorientation caused by the emptying out of the substantial content of our various traditions, to that extent do we become aware of the nature of our crisis. To the extent that we experience the anguish of groping for relevant answers to the problems of meaning raised by our situation, to that extent we experience crisis. To the extent that we take refuge in past identities and allegiances, or in retrospective and dangerously illusory right or left utopias, to that extent we make a regressive response to the crisis. (Here I am agreeing with Roger Garaudy that we are coming to the end of an "ethic of means." But his assumption that the new ends and aims will reveal themselves in "the old way" is in my opinion a dangerously regressive answer to the crisis challenge.) Here we often see the deeper affinity of religion and politics in the long-standing tendency for conservative and traditional religion to seek alliance with conservatives and even right extremists in politics. To the extent that we eschew repeating formulas and attempt serious steps toward transforming anomie into an authentic sense of direction, to the extent that we are capable of generating models for remaking man and society which do not curtail consciousness and which provide a humane context for human activity, to that extent we start to convert a state of crisis into a genuine revolution. Said Marx in 1845, "the occurrence simultaneously of a change in conditions and human activity can only be comprehended and rationally understood as a revolutionary act."[6] We must state emphatically that neither the West nor the socialist countries have been able to embark so far on this genuine revolution. Its first steps must be steps of the understanding.

Before turning to a closer consideration of this crisis another word of caution will not be amiss. This crisis takes on various forms in our present circumstances. The exacerbation of the generational problem is one form; closely related is the feeling that older institutions—university and church, for example—lack relevance; another is the reluctance of many to enter in to what Max Weber called the "iron cage" of an occupational structure which is a form of secularized and increasingly meaningless asceticism seen by the youth as lacking in substance ennobling to human action and enhancing to personal realization. Political expressions of this crisis are confused and are often best understood as symptomatology rather than as intelligent commentary or response.

It must be emphatically underscored that protest is not in itself the expression of wisdom, and neither does it excuse one from the effort after wisdom. Youth complain —not without justification—that "they see a President whose program is constituted largely of finishing touches to the New Deal, and a Congress unwilling to accept even that."[7] There is no reason to hope that youth will see more promise in the Nixon Era. It is a sober truth that most of our political programs in America or in the Soviet Union are concerned with problems left over from the past. They represent a finishing out of the first Industrial Revolution. Yet they are not just "finishing touches," though they may appear as such to people whose condition combines both youth and affluence. Our youth are understandably impatient with this situation. Yet they have to learn that developing an authentically future-oriented program is not an easy task, and no generation, including their's, will do it without serious and often unexciting work, and this together with people over thirty. History has already demonstrated that protest alone can be as sterile and in fact as reactionary as conformity. It is youth's responsibility that they protest, and on the whole it does them credit. It is our responsibility and that of the dead generations before us that they find the situation as it is, and though it is a difficult thing to change history and man, the present situation should humble us and inspire us to a seriousness we do not often attain. It is both youth's and our responsibility that the youth are so poorly educated in any genuine sense of the word and so naively unrealistic and often demagogic in their groping for means and methods to confront the crisis. Both they and we are called upon to do something about that situation. Now let us attempt to look a little more closely at this crisis.

THE DEEPER CRISIS

When a sociologist looks at society he sees a number of institutionalized contexts for human activities. In these contexts, accepted as somehow natural, men act out the drama of their lives. They pursue goals, and they often enter into conflicts of interest. A society allocates functions, facilities and rewards differentially and separates people out into a gradation of haves and have nots. Materially and psychologically the members of society differ in what stake they have in the scheme of things. A society is an objectified framework of consensually validated expectations encumbent upon men. It is in an important sense an acted out answer to the question: *What are men doing here below?* The question is often not asked directly, but the valued activities and rewarded functions in every society answer the question in fact. The institutionalized and indirect answer is highly normative. The institutions of a society represent an answer to the question of what is man doing here below in the sense of *what ought he to be doing, being the kind of being that he is.* Every society is an acted out answer to the fundamental question of man's ontology—what is human existence—what is man's being? Moreover, the religion of a society always—though at times more indirectly than at others—supplies the ultimate grounding, or in Max Weber's word, the legitimation of the society's institutions. In legitimating the society's institutions it legitimates the indirect answer given to the central question of man's meaning.

The sociologist sees this kind of society giving preferential treatment to favored kinds of human activity as evolving in a concrete situation. A society represents a solution to a basic ecological problem. The way in which people solve such problems as to how to provide food and fibre, how to establish and maintain order, and how to achieve other satisfactions establishes normative precedents. The indirect answer to the question of what is man doing is worked out in the solution of the problem of living in a given environment. The forms of the answer—the values of the society— are therefore historically specific. Thus a society is an organized way of performing a set of tasks, (a "division of labor"), an established differential evaluation of kinds of human activities, a legitimated system of differential rewards, and an indirect, acted out answer to the question of man's purpose upon the earth.

The environmental tasks which provide the foci and setting for the development of society are epistemologically complicated, since the mind of man is not simply a mirror (as Marxism seems too often to assume) reflecting unambiguously messages from the environment. The tasks of the environment are based upon realities external to human consciousness, but the understanding of both the environment and the challenges it issues to people differs in different cultures and in different epochs. But we may summarize a subtle but fundamental sociological insight by saying that men make themselves unconsciously and define for themselves what is worthwhile in the course of meeting problems placed before them by their situations.

When we look at European history over the long run in these terms we note a remarkable phenomenon. Western European civilization arose in the early Middle Ages in response to the problem of food and fiber and the problems of order which were severe problems in Europe after the end of the Roman Empire. But it arose in a very real sense within the church. It arose in the intellectual and spiritual atmosphere of a community of withdrawal from the world which was carried over from antiquity. The church taught and propagated its values to the men who were engaged in the solution of the situational problems of survival and development. The church had by this time become highly institutionalized in creed, in liturgy and in hierarchical structure. It defined its own function as mediation between God and man in a two-levelled universe. It saw itself continuing the "high priestly function" of the Christ of the *Epistle to the Hebrews* and relating man to God through the sacraments in the spirit of the Fourth Gospel. As a consequence, while our European ancestors in the 10th and 11th centuries worked out the solution to difficult environmental problems, they accepted a definition of what man should be doing here below of a pronounced other-wordly character. Men here below were on probation for a better and more abundant life in the world beyond. They could win this prize by moral conduct aided by grace which enabled them to share in the salvation purchased by Christ. The chief task of man on earth was to gain his eternal salvation. The church was the institution which embodied this basic answer to the meaning of man; it was the means of achieving man's central task.

What we in the West call the "secularization of culture" is a complex process modifying in thought and in action—and in social institutions—this other-wordly answer to the fundamental question. It often involved a struggle against the church, which like all human institutions defended its *raison-d'être*, the legitimacy of its central function. Such a defensive response always involves for any institution the defense of vested interests.

The process of secularization developed out of European man's experience. New activities came to be valued, and new elites performing them came forward as rivals and competitors of the clergy, the elite of the older other-wordly ecclesiastical function. New activities and new elites meant changes in the texture of consciousness, in the modes of experience, in the perspective upon the world—and consequently in basic value emphases. New implicit answers to the fundamental question came gradually into Western consciousness. I have tried elsewhere to present five strategic contexts in which these developments took place.[8] In raising food and fibre—in "work"—European man tended to develop increased rational mastery over the physical environment. Medieval Europe—unlike the caricature long held about it in modern times—was a period of rapid technological advancement.[9] By the year 1300, Western Europe was as advanced technologically as was the world of classical antiquity at its height. By the excommunication of Luther in 1521, Western Europe was the most technologically advanced society the world had ever known. Increased human control over the environment was a source of secularization.

Early Medieval Europe faced a problem of order which was far more difficult even than that of sustenance. As a consequence, there slowly developed civil government and the rediscovery of Roman Law and its utilization in the building of secular legal and governing institutions. Government and rational legal activity provided another context for developing secularization. The ruling elite was the first new elite to struggle for autonomy of thought and behavior against the established ecclesiastical context. War, the first new elite to struggle for autonomy of thought and the always enticing activity for acting out human dramas of aspiration and meaning, also provided a strategic context for the development of increased rational mastery. Military engineering was the first developed form of engineering, and many advances made in war were only later applied to productive activities. The establishment of order was conducive to the development of commerce. It is interesting to note that despite the official other-worldliness of the European outlook, the European city in the early Middle Ages arose as a commercial venture. This stands in contrast to the sacral origin of the city of antiquity—the *polis* and the *civitas*.[10] The late 11th century saw the beginning of a commercial revolution which in a basic sense has never stopped. In the late 18th century it provided the setting and the stimulus for the Industrial Revolution. Commerce—rational calculation of the future, rational coordination of activities, and rational pursuit of self-interest—had a most thorough transforming influence on the mentality of the rising middle classes. It was a powerful factor making for secularization.[11]

In the 13th century the European university came into existence. It became a unique sociological phenomenon providing a privileged context for thought and discussion. It was to eventuate in the breaking of the clerical monopoly of the things of the mind and spirit and to be important in the development of science. The university, humanistic learning and science would provide a tremendous support and stimulus for secularization and give rise to a new elite to rival the clergy even upon their own ground. In each of these contexts a rationalization of life and a secularization of thought took place; in each of these a new lay elite engaged in this-worldly tasks, acting out this-worldly dramas of self-realization here and now, evolved as rivals to the older clerical elite with its now hardened other-worldly ideology.

How did the church respond to these developments? The church was at times a force for secularization and at

times a barrier against it. In some respects the church en-
couraged—even initiated—these developments; in others
it bitterly resisted them. But a long term historical judgment is possible. The fact is that the church—the Christian thinkers whose task it was to comprehend and maintain a deeper relevance—did not really come to grasp
what was taking place in this long developmental process.
That is not necessarily said in criticism; it may have been
too early in the process to be able to look back and comprehend in depth what was taking place and what was in
the making. The vocabularly of classical philosophy as
taken over by the church was not clearly adequate to the
task. Men groped blindly amid great transformations and
fought bitterly the differences between them to which the
great changes gave rise. Christianity did not see the challenge to its central premises implicit in these developments. It managed to adapt on the surface level, at times
more creatively than at others, but the intellectual and
spiritual initiative slipped gradually from Christians as
Europe entered the modern period.

Another way of describing the background of our present situation is to say that we are involved in what Raymond Williams calls the "long revolution."[12] Williams
sees three aspects of this revolution as significant over the
long run. There is first of all the secular trend toward
democratization. This takes its origin far in the past. Over
a century ago de Tocqueville saw the United States of the
1830's as the forwardmost thrust of this historic tendency.
It is also what Hegel in the early 19th century characterized as the tendency toward the universal and homo-
geneous state. The second secular trend making up the
long revolution is the Industrial Revolution. This development comes after a long period of confused prepara-

tion and actually reaches the point of take-off around 1786.[13] It has led to a complete transformation of man and culture. It uprooted populations, put an end to isolated rural provincialisms and turned us all into urbanized modern men. It is now spreading to the entire globe. Williams sees these two intricately intertwined historical developments related to a third and more profound aspect of the long revolution—related to an even deeper transformation. He speaks of this as the "cultural revolution." It consists of a pervasive and continuing change in the way man experiences the world, in the way in which he apprehends and apperceives the meaning of existence. In our day it represents a culmination of the changes in the Western mentality developing down through the centuries to which we stand heir. Williams says, "Consciousness really does change, and new experience finds new interpretations: this is the permanent creative process. If the existing meanings and values could serve the new energies, there would be no problem."[14] Williams is speaking of Great Britain, but *mutatis mutandis* the problem is a general one in the West and in the Soviet Union as well, for there too the young find the established meanings unable to serve the new creative energies released by technological success.

The modern period of European dominion in the colonies and of world hegemony of the British Empire was one in which important aspects of this long revolution were exported to the non-European world. The end of European colonialism, heralded and hastened by two world wars, has intensified the participation of the "third world" in this great secular process. The result is world-wide instability and at times chaos. The long revolution is becoming a world revolution. The cold war is obviously in significant respects a contest concerning how the new communities which will embody this long revolution will be organized. The chief contestants have been a reformed bourgeois liberalism—often quite reformed—and Marxist socialism. Up till now Christianity has played a lesser role, although it now seems to be facing up to the long term seriousness of some of these questions.[15] Both the East and the West see this struggle in terms of perspectives and conceptions conditioned by their respective history. The West uses "democracy" as a sacral slogan, and the East makes a similar use of the word "socialism." But such logomachy does not often give to either of them any lost key to comprehension of the deeper significance of the long revolution in which we are involved.

Early in his discussion Williams makes an observation palpably true but worthy of note. He states that although this long revolution has taken place over a long period of time, it is a fact that each generation tends to think that it has witnessed its completion. As a consequence, the next generation must pick it up against the wishes and sanctions of the establishment. It must be advanced in protest and rebellion. It is quite significant that successive generations should repeat this astigmatic perception of a historical process in which we have been involved for so long. It is curious that we have not made a more intelligent and more systematic attempt to understand the nature of this transformation. Perhaps it has only now become apparent what is really taking place; possibly only now have we emerged out of our past sufficiently to see the secular trend in some historical perspective; possibly also we have half-consciously tried to avoid facing the dimensions of this long revolution. We have already seen that Western man built Western civilization, conquered and transformed nature, and transformed his way of life and his very selfhood while holding to value-orientations and beliefs about human destiny which did not allow him to develop a clear definition of where he was going. The positive contribution of his earlier heritage to his later achievements have been pointed out often enough. It has been noted that the basic guidelines and fundamental values given him by the Judeo-Christian tradition led him to take history seriously, to see *being as good and to apply his energies to subduing the earth*. It has been observed that his sense of and dedication to progress is to an important degree a secularization of the idea of the messianic age and the fullness of time. His humanism has derived in some important part from the biblical notion of man made in God's image and capable of a relationship with God.

Whitehead has observed that science developed on the assumptions of medieval theology and as a result of the rational discipline to which it subjected the European mind. Collingwood has seen the basic anchorage points of Western thought in the Nicene Creed. These statements all point to the facts of our intellectual and spiritual history. The basic orientation underlying important achievements of Western civilization show a marked intellectual congruence with the basic elements of the religion of the Bible. To borrow the psychoanalytic term, the basic *latent* content of Western culture bears a remarkable similarity to the basic content of biblical religion. This congruity, together with what we know of history, suggests that Western religion has given Western man a complex of values and a sense of direction which influenced tremendously his accomplishments. Writing in 1912, Ernst Troeltsch felt, despite all the secularization of European culture and all the hostility to Christianity, that basic elements shoring up our social system were derived from the Christian heritage. He felt that belief in individual autonomy, in progress, confidence in life and the impulse to work all owed much to that background.[16] Max Weber saw the central motivational structure moving our occupational system as the product of an earlier religiously-oriented motivation.[17]

But that is only part of the picture. This-worldly progress was also won in opposition to the basic religious view of the meaning of man. Though Christianity and Judaism took this world seriously and saw history as the acting out of a divine drama, that apprehension was soon given an otherworldly interpretation. For medieval Catholicism the expectation of the parousia gave way to an emphasis upon a sacramental present relation to God through Christ, and the world was transformed into an arena for the practice of the moral act. Man's life on earth was seen as a short probation for a long eternity. European man's religious outlook and sensitivities, though they prepared him on one level to achieve this-worldly accomplishments, did not in any way prepare him to be able to define realistically what it was he was doing. He saw that only partially. He did one thing and thought what he was doing was something else, or at times saw what he was doing in the world as sinful and regrettable though in some way necessary to the human state. The story is told of King Louis XIV of France, the Sun King whose career represented the epitome of this-worldly ambition, that when he was old and suffering defeats and serious reversals of fortune he said to a confidant, "Few people have experienced the misfortunes which have befallen me," and he added, "God punishes me, but I have well deserved it."[18] The secularization of thought represents a development of realistic this-worldly thinking about man's situation in the world. It developed under the great handicap of having to overcome the otherworldly premises with which it started. This necessity kept it from gaining clarity about what was really happening. Moreover, secular thought developed in conflict with religious thought. One consequence of that situation was that it caused secular thinking to spurn important insights about man contained in the religious tradition and often to become highly distorted by the elements of that ideological struggle.

After the 1660's and during the entire 18th century there took place a decisive secularization of thought on the part of important strata in Western society. In politics and in commerce men pursued this-worldly ambitions and aspirations. In the intellectual sphere men tried to define the answer to the fundamental question of what ought man to be doing more and more in this-worldly terms. Christianity on the whole became increasingly sectarian and defensive in the face of these developments. As we shall see more fully in the next chapter, the basic line of conflict in modern intellectual life became drawn ever more tautly—humanistic and scientific thought versus religion. In politics the new elites asserted their worth, their autonomy and their legitimacy in a bitter conflict with the church. Puritanism had put together a this worldly-orientation with a profound religious conviction that activity in the world was somehow the will of its obscure God. But that view too became secularized and merged with other secular trends.

Unquestionably the most successful attempt to propose a definition of man and his destiny as history was revealing them in practice was Marxism. It was a radical recasting of the ancient Western religious myth, and in some ways it exhibited a remarkable fidelity to the original. The Marxists, following Hegel, saw man working out a destiny here below, a destiny in which he came increasingly to gain self-consciousness in making himself. They saw the older religious definition of what man was doing as a projective dream, at best ennobling man's emotions and consoling him for his deprivations and at worst blinding him to the possibilities of grasping destiny by the forelock and doing something about it. Yet salvation and regeneration, derived from Judeo-Christian messianism, remained central and the Marxists became in important respects secularized evengelicals. In time, though it came to prevail in large parts of the world, Marxism hardened into an ideology which can now be considered to have all the pejorative elements of religious ideologies as perceived by the Marxists.

The deeper religious crisis consists in the fact that our religious tradition no longer provides us with the answer to the profound questions which our contemporary experience elicits from us. Having multiplied and subdued the earth, having at our disposal the capacity to alter our environment, our society and the structure of our selfhood, what ought we to do? We have seen that over a long period our religious tradition failed to provide men with the basis for an adequate understanding of their historical existence. It was oriented to otherworldly aims and goals, and this-worldly values and this-worldly understanding had often to be achieved despite it. The odd askewness of our history in the West consists in the attainment of great political and scientific accomplishments together with a fundamental understanding of man which accorded those achievements little ultimate worth. The develop-

ment of this-worldly philosophies and ideologies long
continued to bear the marks of the older view or of over-
determined rebellion against it, with the consequence that
Western man was never able to achieve an adequate intellectual transcendence or an adequate practical leverage
over his situation to make use of his capacities in his
larger interest. Moreover, Western man's achievements
and his historical experience render him today, by and
large, no longer able to believe in the old way,[19] and his
religious counselors are not able to translate the wisdom
of the tradition into language useful to men of the world.
One serious aspect of this crisis, as we saw in Chapter I,
is that its consequent anomie and disorientation leave
large numbers of people in crises of direction and even
of identity. In this condition Western religion, which
originally opened up the vista of transcendence for mankind, often now becomes a regressive attempt to handle
ideologically the impact of the crisis upon individual
consciousness. One result of this is that for the last two
centuries religion, which should ennoble us and enhance
our interior strength and freedom, has tended to become
deeply involved in sectarian defensive maneuvers, attempting to shore itself up and avoid facing the deeper problems coming to view for large numbers of Western men.
It has been confused in thought and action with those
kinds of conservative and reactionary responses which are
based upon vested interests and regressive fears.[20]

THE DEEPER CRISIS AND OUR GROWING
AWARENESS

We are only now becoming aware of the historically
strategic character of the crossroads at which Western man

stands. In the past men became aware of partial aspects of the deeper condition or felt its effects confusedly and sought confused and at times regressive remedies. The process of secularization slowly won the center of the stage and established the worth and legitimacy of this-worldly values. This movement was in the large "anti-Christian." One consequence of how this tragic division of the Western consciousness into a dialectic of "liberalism" versus "conservatism" took place was that important insights and values on each side tended to be distorted and even lost, and a bitter ideological fight transformed the growth of modernity into a distorted, one-sided reaction against an equally distorted, one-sided religious tradition. Another is to be seen in the fact that there were soon no value-systems securely institutionalized in terms of which general ethical judgments could be made about the new secular activities and their concomitant ideological phenomena coming into existence as modern religion surrogates. Imperialism, nationalism, economically oriented ambitions and the like often took over dominion and became the directing symbols of men's actions. Such ideas became dominant because the elites which embodied them became dominant and because they seemed to offer hope to the frustrated common people. Marx and Engels put it this way:

The bourgeoisie, wherever it has got the upper hand, has put an end to all feudal, patriarchal, idyllic relations. It has pitilessly torn asunder the motley feudal ties that bound man to his "natural superiors," and has left no other nexus between man and man than naked self-interest, than callous "cash payment." It has drowned the most heavenly ecstasies of religious fervour, of chivalrous enthusiasm, of philistine sentimentalism, in the icy water of egotistical calculation. It has resolved personal worth into exchange value, and in place of the numberless indefeasible chartered freedoms, has set up that single, unconscionable freedom—Free Trade. In one word, for exploitation, veiled by religious and poetical illusions, it has substituted naked, shameless, direct, brutal exploitation.

The bourgeoisie has stripped of its halo every occupation hitherto honoured and looked up to with reverent awe. It has converted the physician, the lawyer, the priest, the poet, the man of science, into its paid wage laborers.[21]

This is more prophecy than science; but it points to the direction things were taking. The resulting situation often led to attempts to "remythologize" life to achieve meaning and security in the midst of instability and confusion. The classic case is Nazism.[22] It also led to the ideologization of Marxism, which originally had been an important leap forward for the Western consciousness. The long revolution of which secularization was a salient aspect transformed the texture of Western awareness, while the progress of science and technology (itself a part of the long revolution) uprooted man from provincial stability and traditional values. Man's experience became "demythologized," and too often as a response men sought new and misleading ideologies or desperately clutched their ancient gods. To gain a better vantage point to examine this situation let us look at the period just before the uneasiness and anxieties of the crisis became familiar and everyday phenomena.

In the opening of her book, *The Guns of August,* Barbara Tuchman presents a detailed description of the funeral of King Edward VII.[23] The royalty of Europe and the other leaders of its national communities marching behind the bier of the dead monarch offer more than a spectacle. They present an almost sacramental pageant dramatizing the basic values of the old order which was in four years to be definitively destroyed. But the Europe brought into existence by the process of secularization and the long revolution must never have appeared more secure and indeed more magnificent to its participants as on that occasion. The year was 1910. Economically the world was organized around London; central to its economic structure was the London metropolitan economic and financial community. The core of this was the British Empire, upon which nature's sun never set, and extended beyond the Empire properly so-called to France and the United States as ranking junior partners.[24] Politically and militarily Europe (and particularly Great Britain) "kept order" in the world and subordinated that order to its own economic, political and cultural interests. This was not always simply crude "exploitation," as the new anti-colonial ideologies of the third world would have one believe, but it did establish a lopsided relationship between peoples, and most unfortunately between peoples of different color and different physical characteristics.[25] Science had achieved enormous theoretical advances and changed man's understanding of himself and his world. Here a series of archetypal names come to mind—Sir Charles Lyell, Darwin and Wallace, Koch and Pasteur, etc. Technology had transformed life markedly, and Europe, which had once understood its "superiority" in terms of its "true religion," now saw it as the consequence of a Baconian knowledge which was also power. A semi-religious feeling of cultural and spiritual superiority was present—a feeling that could easily pass over into racism.[26] And what of religion itself? Protestant scholarship, especially in Germany, led the Christian world, but may be said to have contributed as much to confusion reflecting the undermining of the old as to development of a new and relevant Christianity.

On the whole, liberal Protestantism appeared to have achieved a kind of reconciliation with secularization, and Europe's "higher religion" and its "higher civilization" seemed to many to give the adequate and appropriate expression to Western man's vast achievements. Catholicism was a huge defensive sect beneath whose surface rumbled the tremors which were not to surface for almost half a century and seemed secure in its pseudo-monolithic authoritarianism. Jews, in their vast majority, had not yet achieved emancipation, but in the countries of Western Europe they had for some time been integrating themselves into the secularized life of the gentiles. In America, the Eastern European Jew was experiencing freedom and opportunity of an unprecedented kind, and soon (after World War I) Jewry as a whole would be granted formal emancipation. This was the Europe whose nobility Mrs. Tuchman describes so well. It presented an impressive picture, but beneath the surface lay all the problems which were soon to rend its fabric and dispel its illusions. Industrialism in America and Western Europe—and increasingly in Eastern Europe and some of the colonial lands as well—had created problems whose dimensions had not even been guessed—problems which reform in the West had only partially dealt with and which had not been handled at all in the East. An aggressive and able new Germany was challenging the political and commercial hegemony of the London metropolitan community, had topped it in scientific and cultural achievement and would soon shatter the older world in the attempt to topple it militarily.

War, revolution, and the evident development of the dissolution of the world which Europe had built on the basis of industrialism and political and commercial expansion would soon be the condition of Western society. There had been minds earlier who had seen to one degree or another what was happening. There were the early socialists, there was the "scientific socialism" of Marx and Engels. In 1912 the Labor and Socialist International meeting at Basle spoke out against the coming war. Intellectuals of varied stripes showed some awareness of crisis beneath the surface. Tennyson, for example, knew that deep dilemmas existed beneath the calm surface of Victorian thought. Henry George had suggested that perhaps the tide was turning for the West; perhaps it was too early to see it clearly, and we confused the beginning of the ebb with a continuing flood. Others spoke, not always clearly, of the decline of the West or the operation of some kind of law of civilization and decay. Matthew Arnold thought he heard the recession of the tides of faith "down the vast edges drear" of Europe's world.

What of the religious crisis? The religious crisis by 1910 was actually of such long duration, and the compartmentalizations and semi-intentional ambiguities with which it was handled were with us for so long, that no one noticed it much. For the dominant classes, the elites, the cultured, religion was mostly a complex of attenuated memories, ethical and aesthetic. For the middle classes religion remained important, more so in America than in Europe, but it was a religion that compromised itself with what was often a banal secularity. In Western Europe the working classes of the new industrial system left the church and went to Marxism for their community and ideology. In America, the Irish, immigrants from the oppressed enclave of London's nearest submerged suburb, kept Catholicism alive and indeed vigorous.[27] What did educated Europe and America believe in 1910? What was the religion of the strategic decision-making elements of the West in 1910? What was the relation of what the various churches taught to the experience which engendered the optimism of that time? What would the church do when the optimism would soon vanish like a morning mist before the rising sun? Religion was obviously not at all prepared to understand the profound character of the crisis about to break in upon the self-satisfaction of the bourgeois world.

Then came the war. The four years that followed were, as Graham Wallas wrote, 'four years of the most intense and heroic effort the human race has ever made.' When the effort was over, illusions and enthusiasms possible up to 1914 slowly sank beneath a sea of massive disillusionment. For the price it had paid, humanity's major gain was a painful view of its own limitations.

The proud tower built up through the great age of European civilization was an edifice of grandeur and passion, of riches and beauty and dark cellers. Its inhabitants lived, as compared to a later time, with more self-reliance, more confidence, more hope; greater magnificence, extravagance and elegance; more careless ease, more gaiety, more pleasure in each other's company and conversation, more injustice and hypocrisy, more misery and want, more sentiment including false sentiment, less sufference of mediocrity, more dignity in work, more delight in nature, more zest. The Old World had much that has since been lost, whatever may have been gained. Looking back on it from 1915, Emile Verhaeren, the

Belgian Socialist poet, dedicated his pages, 'With emotion, to the man I used to be.'[28]

D. H. Lawrence said, "All the great words were cancelled out for that generation." The West unleashed a war upon itself whose pursuit was to reveal its lack of spiritual and ideational mooring. Let me offer this one quotation from George F. Kennan:

As for the Western peoples and their passionate preoccupation with the issues of World War I, I would not wish to wander too far into the realm of controversy. What is at issue here is, of course, the soundness of the Allied cause in the latter stages of that war, as the Allied peoples and governments then conceived it. There can of course be many views about this. No one would wish to belittle the huge fund of idealism, courage, and good faith that was invested in the war on the Allied side in those final months. Nor would I wish to suggest that the German problem was not an important problem in its own right. It was then; it still is today.

But I wonder whether anyone can read today the literature emanating from the Western countries in the final year of World War I without feeling that he is in the presence of a political hysteria so violent that the real outlines of right and wrong, in so far as they may ever have existed at all, are largely lost in the turmoil. In the bewilderment that accompanied this hysteria, two mistakes were made. First, the significance of the German problem was inflated out of all semblance of reality. The Germans were a problem in Europe —yes; but they were not as awful a problem as all this: their guilt for the outbreak of the war was not *so* great, their victory would not have been quite *such* a catastrophe, nor would *so* many problems be solved by their defeat. But an even more serious error was the failure to recognize the limitations of modern war generally as a means to an end—the failure to realize to what extent prolonged warfare in the industrial age, with its fearful expenditure of blood and substance, was bound to be self-defeating.

The things people thought they were trying to achieve by the long and terrible military exertion in Europe were simply not to be achieved by this means. The indirect effects of that war—its genetic and spiritual effects—were far more serious than people realized at the time. We can see, today, that these effects penalized victor and vanquished in roughly equal measure, and that the damage they inflicted, even on those who were nominally the victors, was greater than anything at stake in the issues of the war itself. In other words, it did not take the atom to make warfare with modern weapons a fruitless and self-defeating exercise. This was already a reality in 1918; and the recognition of this offers, in my opinion, the key to the understanding of a great deal of the subsequent history of the Western peoples.

This is what I mean when I say that the conflict the Allies were interested in at the time of the Russian Revolution was one about which they were largely wrong, just as the Bolsheviki were wrong about theirs. The same could, of course, be said of the Germans, though to a lesser degree. In the later stages of the war the Germans, I think, saw things somewhat more clearly than did people in the Allied countries, partly because they had never had such a sense of virtue about the war from the beginning, partly because they were now more disillusioned with it and hoped for less from it. But both sides hoped for more than could really be achieved. Both underestimated the seriousness of the damage they were doing to themselves—to their own spirit and to their own physical substance—in this long debauch of hatred and bloodshed.[29]

I do not quote this because I consider Kennan some kind of oracle, or because I necessarily agree with his evaluation. Historical revisionism and reconsideration of these great matters of World War I and II and of the origin of the cold war are now in full force. But no matter what view we take of these developments, the basic fact of concern here emerges. Western man was bereft of a definition of what he was doing which could prove serviceable in the prevention of catastrophe, or in stopping it once it had started, or in recovering from it once it had run its course.

The war came. It was handled badly, and it left in its wake untold physical suffering and spiritual desolation. Marx had said earlier that the last heroic effort of which the old society was capable was war. Now war had proven its undoing.

Europe's success in building a great lay civilization placed enormous capacity at the disposal of the Great Powers. The political situation was a complex one, and no international machinery existed which could serve as a useful context for handling conflicts once they arose. Without such machinery, the system of alliances made it almost a certainty that serious crisis would lead to war. The point stressed here, however, is this: the lack of a realistic philosophical basis for understanding what it had really accomplished and what capabilities it placed at men's command, the lack of a realistic view of his needs and potentialities, left European man without guidance. What man believed ultimately about himself, or said he believed ultimately about himself, made little contribution to the kind of comprehension of man and his condition needed at that time. Liberalism—the secularization of the older Judeo Christian-Hellenic view—might supply slogans and Christianity consolation, but what the world needed was a wisdom that reflected the facts of man's Western development.

It is interesting in this respect to note that developing nations pass through two periods in which a sober and realistic basis for decision-making is especially crucial. In his paradigmatic outline of this process, W. W. Rostow points out that as the point of possible take-off is approached and the economy builds up a surplus available for investment, the problem of how this surplus shall be utilized arises. The answer given to that question depends upon the social structure of the society, the motivational disposition of its decision-making elites, and the ideas and values in terms of which aims and goals are set. It is common, Rostow points out, for the surplus to be used in military adventures. War has long been an important method for the acting out of human aspirations and needs —for power, for glory, for self-expression, for defense, for enhancement, for self-validation. The attraction of military adventures is increased by the ideological and indeed "quasi-religious" character of nationalism. It derives also from certain realities of power in a relatively unorganized world, but the problems here are exacerbated by the ideological element which gives a "quasi-ultimacy" to competitions and rivalries. In our day, the Middle East is one—but only one—area of the world where these conditions are to be seen. Rostow further notes that after the maturation of an industrial economy and an unprecedentedly large surplus is now at the society's disposal, the problem arises anew and on a vaster scale. There is involved here an additional problem of knowledge. Rostow suggests, for example, that by the 1851 Crystal Palace Exposition, Great Britain had already reached economic maturity. He defines such maturity as that technological condition in which a society is capable of making a wide choice in the use of its great productive capacities. But it was not recognized for a long time what kind of powers men had actually achieved. After a discussion of the internal structural problems which maturity brings about in a society, Rostow says:

These changes in the real income, structure, ambitions, and outlook of a society, as maturity comes to be achieved, pose a searching problem of balance and choice around the question: how shall this mature industrial machine, with compound interest built into it, be used? To offer increased security, welfare and perhaps leisure for the citizens as a whole? To offer enlarged real incomes, including the manufactured gadgets of consumption, to those who can earn them? To assert the stature of the new mature society on the world scene?[30]

Maturity can also be a dangerous time. The temptations of glory and the "choice of aggression" become real options.[31] As Europe advanced into maturity it failed to see the true dimensions of what was coming to be. Economic science, developed as the science of allocation of scarce means in conditions of chronic scarcity, was not ready with the kinds of conceptualizations which could be of help, and what Galbraith has called the "conventional wisdom" of our leaders was little better.[32] Consequently it was not until after a second bloody war that the peaceful possibilities of the new situation came to have some general recognition. The West approached industrial maturity unprepared either by its science or by its basic beliefs and values to meet the new problems. The surplus has been squandered in two world wars and in innumerable lesser adventures, and is still consumed far too much in the maintenance of the establishments of war and defense.

The questions now are these: Having reached industrial maturity, what shall we do with our productive capacity? Having now the capacity to control our environment, we have by the same token the ability to make ourselves— to assume an unprecedented degree of self-direction. How shall we use this new capacity? To answer these questions we shall have to determine some basis for setting up preferences and priorities, and to do that we shall have to arrive at some degree of self-comprehension and achieve in relation to self-comprehension a sense of direction. The answers cannot be derived from simple utilitarianism. Nor will they be generated from that kind of "buy anything" mentality which sees no irony in our consuming in order to keep working—working at anything. Nor do the circumstances of life in the advanced countries automatically reveal the historically appropriate next steps, as many Marxists pretend to be the case. Our circumstances reveal many unfinished problems from the past, but the new issues must be discovered from an understanding of ourselves and our historical situation. Our basic value-system points to some leads, indeed to some important leads, in helping us to define the dimensions of man to be sustained and the potentialities to be brought to realization.[33] But it does not provide a clear basis for choice and decision, nor a clear justification for choices arrived at and decisions made.

The fact that our basic world view and our basic definition of the meaning of man's destiny were for so long profoundly other-worldly has left us at the deeper levels confused about the meaning of a this-worldly destiny. The fact that our this-worldly ideologies came into existence in a conflict with our older religious views impressed upon the former an anti-traditionalism, and often a militant and superficial anti-traditionalism, which kept them from examining profoundly the questions of human destiny central to the older view. Man's this-worldly role was taken as "self-evident" and simply asserted. This historical conflict established a dialectic in which two partial insights, both partly right and partly wrong (and necessarily so by their very partial character), both leaving out important aspects of man in their definitions of him, more and more took on rigid ideological form and became the cause of conflict. Moreover, interests of a profound character, both psychological and material, got bound up with this conflict—as is always the case.

THE PROBLEM FOR AMERICA

To survey briefly the application of this discussion to the American situation, I shall turn to statements I have written elsewhere.[34] "American history reveals two major historical "tasks" around which American society has developed and its values and social structure evolved. First we find the task of agriculture and Westward movement, upon the basis of which the early United States was built. Next we find Industrialization and the result of it, urbanization. In the century from the Civil War to our own day it was this second great task of building up the American industrial base which occupied the central attention and the greater energies of our countrymen. America was transformed from an agricultural to an industrial nation. Now in the two decades after World War II, service industry is replacing basic industry as a chief focus of occupational energies. We are evolving a service economy—with mixed public and private sectors—as the basic infrastructure of a welfare state.

"An important social process is seen to be intimately and intricately bound up with these basic economic activities—the reception and assimilation of immigrants into the American society. Moreover, the republican and democratic forms which America evolved as an agrarian nation have been preserved and even strengthened. In setting out upon these tasks American society possessed two sources of strength which differentiated it from the older societies of Europe. It had the advantage of new ground—a vast continent endowed with rich resources and unencumbered by the time-honored precedents of countless generations. Yet even Frederick Jackson Turner, who emphasized the importance of the Frontier in the making of American institutions and American character, was quite aware that the ideas and values which men brought to the settlement of the new areas were of great significance in affecting the social and cultural outcome of American settlement. But here too there were elements which strengthened the anti-traditionalist effects of new ground. In the Calvinism of New England we find Christianity recast in a form suitable to find resonance in the mentalities of rising middle classes, a Christianity supportive of work in the world and of commercial activity—the strategic form of work in the world in that era—and shorn of its earlier sacramental and passive receptive characteristics. Puritanism is perhaps the most rational this-worldly formulation of Christian asceticism and the most anti-traditional form of Christianity to be developed by the Reformation period. It represented an important ideological and psychological break with traditionalism. In a different but related way, those elements of Anglicanism in Virginia which led to Deism and the consequent acceptance of the developing

English Liberal ideology must also be counted as important non-traditional influences in our history.

"It was out of this kind of colonial background that America developed. The people of the new republic essayed their tasks supported by two general kinds of ideology, denominational Protestantism which was evolving out of the earlier situation of established colonial (and later, in some places, state) churches,[35] and the Lockean Liberalism with French touches of the Deists of Virginia and the evolving Congregationalists of Massachusetts. Protestantism was effective on the frontier (to a considerable extent because of the efforts of the Methodists), important in the rural areas of a country dominantly agricultural in its occupational structure, and was the religion of the old stock and the middle and the upper classes. Liberalism made its headway among the educated, and the second half of the 19th century saw Protestantism, which had gained much ground in the first half, slowly give way before a growing secularization of culture.[36] In church and university the latter part of the 19th century saw conflict between conservative and liberal forces and between supporters of secularization and advocates of an earlier religious dominance. Catholicism, insignificant before the Irish and German immigrations of the 1840's, came in as the religion of immigrants, of ethnic groups (seen as foreigners), of lower and working classes which came increasingly to be made up of the newcomers and their children.

"W. W. Sweet has stated that Catholicism played a significant part in providing a meaningful orientation and a spiritual home for millions of immigrants and was a most important support of public order in an era of great change and hardship, and potentially of great social disruption. Protestantism, by and large, split into a liberal and a fundamentalist sector, and secular liberalism to one extent or another made important headway among the sophisticated, though a vague Protestant connection or at least identity remained part of the self-definition of most old stock Americans. Catholicism was highly affected by the openness and liberalism of its new surroundings. The 19th century was a time of brisk and significant conflict in American Catholicism as a vigorous immigrant community adapted itself to an entirely new kind of society.[37] The general Modernist crisis in Catholicism and the condemnation of the Americanist heresy, the defeat of "Trusteeism" (a form of lay control fought and defeated by the hierarchy) and the generally unpropitious atmosphere for Catholicism in the 19th century led eventually to a tamed but highly Americanized version of conservative European Catholicism which remained typical of America to the eve of the Second Vatican Council.

"These two basic tasks upon which American society was constructed gave rise to three great struggles. The first was the continued Westward settlement—a saga of heroism, but also a tale of brutal exploitation of land, resources and fellowmen and racist violence against the aborigines. The second derived from the two different kinds of societies and value systems which were built in North and South on the basis of two vastly different forms of agriculture—one based upon an independent yeomanry, the other upon the plantation and slavery. The unsolved problems of the Civil War and its aftermath remain with us as America tries after a century of callous neglect to do something about its racial problems. Today this issue becomes related to and entangled with that of the assertion of independence and the struggle for viable nation-hood by the non-white peoples of the globe, but in the American setting it is a problem left over from the past. It is an urgent problem but it is hardly a new one. The second task—industrialization—and its consequence, ur-banization, was also a relatively violent affair. It was closely related to the assimilation of the immigrant. It gave rise to a considerable number of important reactions as group after group felt their interests and even their survival threatened. The farmers, victims of the agricul-tural market and its fluctuations and disadvantaged by the new large-scale capitalism, founded several movements—the grange, the farmers' alliances, the populists and the progressives. Workers developed a trade union movement against great repressive opposition—the National Labor Union, The Knights of Labor, the American Federation of Labor, and the Congress of Industrial Organizations. There also came into existence a radical left—a socialist party and such an anarcho-syndicalist movement as the I.W.W. From the more public spirited sections of the city middle classes came agitation and movements advocating governmental reform. Movements for good government attempted to curtail the rampant corruption which a vigorous, expansive and unscrupulous capitalism had in-troduced into political life.

"In the administration of Grover Cleveland, the Federal Government set up the Interstate Commerce Commission. It was weak in powers, but it symbolized much that was to come. Since then the establishment of numerous gov-ernment regulatory agencies, the growing socio-economic concern of Congressional legislation, and the response of the Federal Government to social and resource problems slowly introduced a measure of social responsibility into the new economic structure that was emerging. Government regulation, a reformed tax structure of which a graduated income tax was a most significant innovation, strong labor and collective bargaining together with what has often been called the "managerial revolution" in the structure of industry have transformed the basic economic substructure of American society. The years following World War II saw a vastly increased prosperity with the development of a consumer-oriented service economy, and saw this prosperity spread among an unprecedentedly large section of the total American population. Education tended to become democratized, and educational attainment became the chief route to social and economic mobility. Meanwhile America continued to play the role in international affairs which it reluctantly started to perform in 1917 when it entered the Great War on the side of the Allied Powers. This international role continues, and continues to be a main source of disagreement and internal conflict among Americans.

"These two basic tasks and their many derivatives in city, town and farm have provided the basic setting for American efforts for decades. American man has made himself in this work—his settlement of the continental expanse and his construction upon it of an advanced technologically-based society. In the process he has preserved his basic democratic institutions in altered form and his older ideologies, often much transformed. Today this American man faces two sets of problems. First are those derived from or left over from the two basic tasks which occupied him in history up to now—renovation of cities, justice to minorities, the structurally and spiritually dispossessed poor who cannot become part of the affluent

society. This is the first set of problems; they represent
a continuation of the tasks of the past. They are serious
and urgent but they are hardly *avant garde*. Beneath these
problems lurk the deeper, more radical, and more significant problems—the problems not left over from yesterday
but awaiting us on the morrow. What kind of society are
we going to make with the great powers our learning and
science, our past accomplishments and successes have
placed at our disposal? How now, with our scientific
leverage over our situation and ourselves, are we to pro-
ceed toward self-realization and a society conducive to
humane self-realization? A Christian and later a secular
utopianism often inspired our ancestors—America was
the "last best hope" of mankind, and Americans in Lincoln's words were God's "almost chosen people." Here on
this continent we would realize the long thwarted aspirations of men for a humane and significant life. How shall
we give substance to that vision today? The question
"what is man doing on this earth?" in a sense of what
ought he to be doing now becomes a question which is
to be found lurking beneath every problem and conflict
in our current situation.

"The identity crises of many of our youth,[38] the religious
crisis of our time,[39] the tendency for many to seek a
symbolic security in a radicalism of the right[40] and much
of the groping and seeking of our day are closely related
to and indeed part of this deeper set of problems. Under
these circumstances many seek what in effect are repressive modes of handling this basic crisis, of concealing
from themselves the urgency of this problem. They seek
modes in older causes and identities often stridently
asserted and often quite symbolically and unrealistically

perceived and formulated. Others manage to live, not altogether comfortably in halfway houses, concerning themselves with the more immediate set of problems while avoiding the deeper questions which cannot be conjured away. The churches and the universities—the guardians of our religious and humane traditions—must begin to face up to what is involved here. The university becomes an ever more central institution in our total society involved in many ways in the most diverse public and private enterprises. To be true to itself, it must take the lead in the human effort to understand man and to enable man to achieve genuine humanity. For the churches, their ability to render relevant support to this venture will test their meaning for the new world that must be built."

We are indeed in the middle of a religious crisis. It is a religious crisis which represents perhaps the most profound area of confusion and concern in the general consciousness—a crisis of identity and direction—characteristic of the West in our day. It is important that we attempt to comprehend this crisis, and in comprehending it to make available to ourselves the genuine riches of the religious tradition. Religion was for long the most profound area of life in which man projected himself—his fears and hopes, his felt relationships to his world, his relation to his fellows. The religious traditions of mankind reveal much that must not be lost as we essay the task of facing up to our contemporary crisis and approach the points of future decision. We are becoming aware of what modernity means. It means that man becomes problematic to himself, not simply theoretically but also practically. It means that man must confront the crisis of our time which may be a crisis of growth, as is optimistically suggested by the Vatican II,[41] but which without intelligent human intervention could become a crisis of vast destruction. It means that man must confront the crisis of his understanding of himself. It is a crisis to which both religious and educational institutions do not yet make adequate responses. Lewis Mumford has said: "Man does not merely exist as an organic product: he makes something of himself, and that making of man is the meaning of history."[42] Man acts out a drama of self-realization as conditions permit and in terms of his accumulated culture and the demands of his conditions. We now transcend the demands of conditions more than ever before in man's time. We have reached the place in our development as a species where it is no longer adequate to understand our history—our acting out and making of ourselves—ideologically. We have passed by the place where to make history ideologically is safe.

FOOTNOTES

1. See Sidney E. Mead, *The Lively Experiment* (New York: Harper, 1963).

2. See especially G. W. F. Hegel, *The Phenomenology of Mind,* Sir James Baillie, tr. (New York: Humanities, 1964).

3. Karl Marx, Third Thesis on Feuerbach, quoted from Frederick Engels, *Feuerbach; The Roots of Socialist Philosophy,* Austin Lewis, tr. (Chicago, 1903).

4. Quoted from a paper given by the writer at the Religion in Education Foundation Seminar on Value Motivation, Carmel Valley, December 27–29, 1967.

5. Karl Marx, quoted from Engels, *op. cit.,* p. 130.

6. *Ibid.*

7. Frederick Richman, "The Disenfranchised Majority," in

Students and Society. An occasional paper published by the Center for the Study of Democratic Institutions (Santa Barbara, California, 1967), p. 4.

8. Thomas F. O'Dea, *Sociology of Religion* (Englewood Cliffs, New Jersey: Prentice-Hall, 1966), pp. 80–90.

9. See for example Lynn White, Jr., *Medieval Technology and Social Change* (New York: Oxford, 1962), and A. C. Crombie, *Medieval and Early Modern Science,* Vols. I and II (Garden City, New York: Doubleday, 1959).

10. Compare for example Max Weber, *The City,* Don Martindale and Gertrud Neuwirth, trs. and eds. (Glencoe, Illinois: Free Press, 1958), and N. D. Fustel de Coulanges, *The Ancient City* (Garden City, New York: Doubleday, 1950).

11. See Max Weber, *The Theory of Social and Economic Organization,* A. M. Henderson and Talcott Parsons, trs. (New York: Oxford, 1947) for a discussion of the relation of economic activity to the rationalization of life.

12. Raymond Williams, *The Long Revolution* (New York: Columbia, 1961).

13. See for example, Walt W. Rostow, *The Process of Economic Growth,* rev. ed. (New York: Norton, 1960), and *The Stages of Economic Growth* (Cambridge, England: Cambridge University Press, 1960); and T. S. Ashton, *The Industrial Revolution 1760–1830* (New York: Oxford, 1948); Asa Briggs, *The Making of Modern England, 1783–1867* (New York: Harper, 1960).

14. Raymond Williams, *op. cit.,* p. 353.

15. Especially can this be seen in the "Pastoral Constitution on the Church in the Modern World" and in certain encyclicals of the reigning Pope, as that on developing nations and of course in the "Pacem in Terris" of John XXIII. Cf. also many statements of the World Council of Churches.

16. Ernst Troeltsch, *Christian Thought and Its Applications.* New York: Meridian, 1957, p. 60.

17. Max Weber, *The Protestant Ethic and the Spirit of Capitalism,* Talcott Parsons, tr. (New York: Scribner, 1948).

18. Quoted from Henri Daniel-Rops, *The Church in the Seventeenth Century,* Vol. I. (New York: Dutton, 1963), p. 301.

19. I have, of course, discussed this point in chapter one. For

a fuller discussion, see my *The Catholic Crisis* (Boston: Beacon Press, 1968).

20. For example see E. E. Y. Hales, *Pio Nono* (Garden City, New York: Doubleday, 1962) for an account of the "alliance" of religious and political conservatism in 19th century Catholicism, and for the American scene see Richard Hofstadter, *The Paranoid Style in American Politics* (New York: Knopf, 1965).

21. Karl Marx and Frederick Engels, "The Communist Manifesto," quoted from *Handbook of Marxism,* Emile Burns, ed. (New York, 1935), p. 25.

22. See for example Erich Fromm, *Escape from Freedom* (New York: Holt, 1941).

23. Barbara W. Tuchman, *The Guns of August* (New York: Macmillan, 1962).

24. Cf. Robert K. Lamb, "Political Elites and the Process of Economic Development," in *The Progress of Underdeveloped Areas,* B. F. Hoselitz, ed. (Chicago: Chicago University Press, 1952), pp. 30–53.

25. One gets a very good feel of this by reading the two volumes of Nehru's autobiography and such works as Philip Woodruff, *The Men Who Rule India,* Vols. I and II (New York: Schocken, 1964).

26. See Hannah Arendt, *The Origins of Totalitarianism* (New York: Harcourt, 1966).

27. See for example, Robert Cross, *The Emergence of a Liberal Catholicism in America* (Cambridge, Massachusetts: Harvard, 1958), and Thomas N. Brown *Irish-American Nationalism, 1870–1890* (Philadelphia: Lippincott, 1960).

28. Barbara W. Tuchman, *The Proud Tower* (New York: Macmillan, 1965), p. 544.

29. George F. Kennan, *Russia and the West* (Boston: Little Brown and Co., 1961), pp. 8–10. By permission of the Atlantic-Little, Brown and Co. Copyright © 1960, 1961 by James K. Hotchkiss, Trustee.

30. W. W. Rostow, *The Stages of Economic Growth* (Cambridge, England: Cambridge University Press, 1960), p. 72.

31. *Ibid.,* Ch. 8.

32. Cf. John K. Galbraith, *The Affluent Society* (New York:

Houghton, 1958). Galbraith inscribes these words of Alfred Marshall in the beginning of his book, "The economist, like everyone else, must concern himself with the ultimate aims of man."

33. See footnote 15.

34. A paper given at the Religion in Education Foundation Seminar on Value Motivation, Carmel Valley, December 27–29, 1967.

35. Franklin H. Littell, *From State Church to Pluralism* (New York: Aldines, 1962), Sidney E. Mead, *The Lively Experiment* (New York: Harper, 1963).

36. Merle Curti, *The Growth of American Thought,* 3rd ed. (New York: Harper, 1964).

37. Robert D. Cross, *The Emergence of Liberal Catholicism in America* (Cambridge, Massachusetts: Harvard, 1958), and E. E. Y. Hales, *The Catholic Church in the Modern World* (Garden City, New York: Doubleday, 1958).

38. Kenniston, *op. cit.*

39. See chapter one, "The Crisis of the Contemporary Religious Consciousness."

40. Richard Hofstadter, *The Paranoid Style in American Politics* (New York: Knopf, 1965).

41. See: "Pastoral Constitution on the Church in the Modern World."

42. Lewis Mumford, *The Conduct of Life* (New York: Harcourt, 1951), p. 37.

III

Christianity, Humanism and Science

> Whatever the world thinks, he who hath not
> much meditated upon God, the human mind
> and the *summum bonum* may possibly make
> a thriving earthworm, but will most indubi-
> tably make a sorry patriot and a sorry states-
> man.
>
> —Bishop Berkeley

Christianity, humanism and science, closely related and
often interdependent in the course of our history but also
antagonistic in significant respects, have long provided
Western man with his knowledge of himself and with
the ideas and attitudes with which he has related himself
to his world. From none of these can he today derive adequate guidance to meet the new situation which his
enormous scientific and technological advancement has
created for him. Christianity, humanism and science
indeed, each in its own characteristic way, has been one-
sided in its perspective upon existence and consequently
each has, again in its own way, provided Western man
with knowledge which was partial and with orientation
in important ways deficient. In all three of these Western
modes of apprehending the basic reality of the human

condition there have been present elements of "false consciousness." These three have led man, but they have also misled him. Moreover, to develop personal orientations for their own lives men have individually put parts of all three together, but the results produced were never adequate and are now less adequate than ever.

It is this situation which I shall seek to discuss in this chapter. The theme of this book, obviously, is that religion, though in many respects still vital, is in a state of severe crisis. The thrust of this chapter is that the humanities—our contemporary inheritors of the humanistic tradition—are, despite the richness of many fields of humanistic studies, in a state of disarray and confusion, and their practitioners are puzzled to discover their relevance in the contemporary world. Religion and the humanities live today in the house built by science and industry and the conditions of life within it keep both of them off balance.

In our own day government becomes an important element in that picture, taking over, coordinating and organizing much that was previously done by science and industry. Some of this coordination seeks to insure economic growth, though often uncritically; some of it seeks to solve long lasting social evils in our society. But much of it is organized around building a war machine or, as we prefer to say, a defense establishment. Our society is coming to look something like the one imagined early in the 19th century by Auguste Comte. It is becoming a large social system configurated around a central industry-government-education complex. Over the long term period of this development, religion has more and more been rendered secondary, more and more turned into a thing more affected than affecting. In sociological jargon it has become a "dependent variable." Much the same can be said for the humanistic studies.

Yet in past periods of history, religion and humanism have possessed genuine initiative. The Europe that was built upon the ruins of classical antiquity was not just elaborated out of the experience of solving the severe ecological problems which European man faced—the problems of sustenance and of order. It was also built upon the Judeo-Christian and Graeco-Roman traditions which the church and such of an intelligentsia as the church could salvage transmitted to the later age. Marx assumed that religion and the humanities would always be dependent variables—superstructures of thought derived from immediate experience in coping with the environment and the social relations such coping brought into existence. Weber, on the other hand, in a somewhat oversimplified study, demonstrated that religious attitudes can also have a causal role in history. In the last two centuries, however, both religion and the humanities have been forced by developing circumstances increasingly to relinquish any genuine determinative role in the development of modern society. Yet our present technological capacity makes it more and more important that we occupy ourselves again with those problems of man's ultimate meaning which are the concern of religion and the closely related questions of the significance of man and his works treated in the humanities. Yet the elements of false consciousness in religion and the humanities together with their residual relation to those areas of life where the future is being made make it difficult for them to aid man in this predicament.

THE CONTEMPORARY CRISIS

People experience crisis when the past has inadequately prepared them to handle a future which is all but upon them. It is precisely this inadequacy which is characteristic of religion and the humanities today. Religion is a dimension of man's consciousness which is concerned with his ultimate relation to his world and the elements and forces constitutive of that world, with the meaning he finds in or attributes to his life activities and experiences, and with the direction which he gives his efforts and aspirations. Relation refers to his place in the overarching scheme of things, his "at homeness" or alienation—the ways in which he belongs to his world, form among its forms, and the ways in which he does not belong to it but rather is separate from and stands over against that world and points to an ultimate that is beyond it. Meaning refers to a way of seeing experience and events as related to a "spiritual history"—that is to an interior as well as to an exterior enhancement of man's potential. The problem of meaning asks: Do experiences and events contribute to the attainment of worthwhile goals, the fulfillment of satisfying aspirations, the achievement of a fulfilling identity, or do they threaten, restrict or even destroy these possibilities? Direction refers to the future-oriented character of human awareness. Religion provides an ontologically justified sense of direction.

The central thrust of this book, of course, is that religion no longer contributes an adequate sense of relationship and direction and no longer satisfactorily answers the problem of meaning for large numbers in our society, and particularly for those who occupy strategic decision-making positions within it. No less significant is the fact that religion is also mute before the questions of the young—a point to which we shall return in our final chapters.

What about the humanities? I have already indicated that I mean by the humanities those endeavors devoted to the cultivation and expression of man's intellectual and emotional response to his world. The term refers to culture, not in the anthropological usage but rather as designating self-conscious cultivation after models established in man's spiritual history. It shall mean for us the modern equivalent of what the Greeks called *paideia*. Its first and foremost component is the conscious cultivation of man's intellectual and expressive powers. Its second in our day is the critical transmission of the long cultural tradition of the West and the confrontation of the traditions of non-Western peoples. Models of thinking, models of attitude and response, models of action and models of self-fulfillment—styles of thought, feeling and life—from the past are the concern of the humanities. They are to be understood, to be evaluated, to be appreciated and to be criticized. Moreover, form, style, discipline of feeling and expression, all are part of its concerns. The humanities also, on the basis of this rich past, point toward contemporary creativity. To elicit from man the free but disciplined expression of his many-sided capacities has long been the aim of education in the humanities.

In the past the humanistic studies held before men's eyes an ideal of self-fulfillment or realization of intellectual, artistic and humane *arete* and against such models sought to elicit and develop human potentialities. The humanistic studies long cherished an aristocratic ideal and saw their lessons as beyond the capacity and interests of the mass of men. Yet in both these fields and in the general society tendencies were visible which sought to democratize the humanities, not by vulgarizing their content, but by spreading their contributions more widely among the population. It is true that in the period of industrialization in the West the humanities were often pushed into a residual corner and made to serve other interests. Yet they helped to maintain some degree of genuine civilization despite the spiritual brutalities of the age. Tennyson is as much a part of the 19th century as steam and as necessary to its understanding as Ricardo.

The arrival of mass higher education on the university scene has led to an expansion of the humanities along with everything else in the education establishment. But the problems of relevance became more pronounced. Many professors of the humanities today feel quite justifiably that they offer important contributions to education, but they also feel on the defensive before the sciences, and even the social sciences. There is a tendency to stress narrow research and increased specialization beyond the limits of diminishing returns, which is a kind of wrongheaded way of trying to make the humanities "scientific." Humanists and scientists in the "multi-versity" live in different worlds; the two cultures of C. P. Snow are a fact. It is not clear how to make the humanities relevant to our kind of society, although the human relevance of much of their content—if genuinely and ably presented—seems obvious. The social scientists who, it might be hoped, would bridge the gap between the two cultures often know little about the content of the humanities and are themselves often busy aping the natural sciences as they understand them.

All this is of course caught up in the "publish or

perish" complex which in itself is contrary to the spirit of both the humanities and the sciences and represents the penetration of a vulgar quantitativism into the very heart of our institutionalized intellectual life. In all this the voice of the humanities is a confused one. Sometimes our humanists seem to advocate a cultivated hedonism; sometimes to counsel despair; sometimes to continue outmoded cultural conflicts between humanities and science, between science and religion, and between humanism and religion. And all this activity is more and more based upon a narrowly specialized scholarship whose larger significance too often escapes its practitioners. If the religious trumpet gives an uncertain sound, the lyre of the humanities comes through often as sheer cacophony.

Meanwhile the world built by science and industry becomes ever more complicated. Derek J. de Solla Price has noted that science develops in an exponential way. Our present-day technology based upon this exponentially growing science has become the most significant prime mover of all social change in our time. It raises in the minds of all of us the question of what the future holds. Today a number of groups, scholarly and scientific, are attempting to anticipate what things will be like in the year 2000. A number of important articles on the subject have been written, and some books have appeared, perhaps the most notable being *The Year 2000,* by Anthony J. Wiener and Herman Kahn. In that book they note the most striking single fact about our prospects: "Our very power over nature threatens to become itself a source of power that is out of control."[1]

In the decades immediately ahead we can expect an enormous increase in our already considerable capacity to control nature and alter our environment. Computerization opens up great capabilities in any number of fields from precision production to communications and decision-making. But the computer can only be as wise as we are ourselves, and if it beguiles us we shall indeed beguile it. We have all heard something of the revolution in chemistry. Recently a National Academy of Science committee stated that on the average a new chemical compound is synthesized every five minutes. Bernard Barber states that "somewhere between 30 and 50 percent of the chemical products now on the market were unknown, uneconomic or unavailable 25 years ago."[2] The recent developments with respect to altering the genetic code and the even more recent heart transplants suggest some of the things to be expected from medical and biological technology. Indeed this may be the most productive area of all. Wiener and Kahn note that all major technological advances in the past "have resulted in unforeseen consequences." They express doubt as to the ability of "fallible humans" to make decisions in the problems which these things will bring to confront us.

Perhaps we should remind ourselves here, as a painful parenthesis, that as we prepare to face this challenging future, we do so with a number of the most severe unsolved problems left over from the past. Poverty, the terrible racial injustice to the Negro (and to the Indian, but he has not survived in numbers sufficient to make trouble for his white conquerors), the horror of our cities —these we have not yet faced and solved.

Perhaps we should also remind ourselves that we live in a world where the internationalization of the industrial revolution started by Europeans and Americans now proceeds autonomously. It can be counted upon to continue despite all the severe ideological, economic and social problems which stand in its way. The non-Western world will in its own way go through the experience of secularization and the emptying out of the substance of its traditional culture which the West has experienced in its own history. Ibn Saud many years ago declared that his people could erect and maintain a modern oil industry without loosing their Islamic faith! How wrong he will turn out to be, every observer in the Middle East today can plainly foresee.

At the very foundation of all these developments we must recall that our medical technology has brought it about that we must anticipate in the decades immediately ahead an enormous increase in the earth's population. In some places this will indeed amount to an "explosion." Unless a major change is made affecting population growth, the consequences can become extremely serious. Finally we should note what we all know too well—that the technological revolution has put at our command tremendous capacities for destruction—even for self-destruction.

The attempts to predict the year 2000 began with the extrapolation of trends presently visible together with some awareness of how such present trends might affect each other. It has, however, been increasingly recognized that several futures are possible. R. H. Tawney once observed that history "is a stage where forces which are within human control contend and cooperate with forces which are not." That is precisely our situation today. What technology brings about depends in important degree on human decisions—and human decisions depend in the first place upon human intelligence. W. H. Ferry has pointed out that technology is in itself an ambiguous phenomenon; it has both tonic and toxic consequences, and its use must be subject to restraints imposed by human values. But where will we find these values in the face of the crisis of consciousness with which we are concerned here?

In 1961 the Center for the Study of Democratic Institutions had eight Americans representing the three major religious traditions of this country draw up a statement on American religion. While the resulting document was certainly not uncritical, it did state that religion was making a "significant contribution to American life." Religion was seen as contributing several important elements—"recognizing the mystery of human destiny, sustaining civic ideals and ethical standards, re-enforcing the sense of personal dignity" and, finally, "forming men and women of virtue."[3] It is not my intention to deny these important functions to religion in America. What I do suggest is that these functions were not and are not carried out within the context of an intelligent and realistic appraisal of the problems which we as a society face in our day. Moreover, if it is one consequence to be expected of the humanistic studies that men grow in wisdom, is their record any better than that of religion? After all, the managerial revolution is a fact. The route to social mobility is no longer so much the reinvestment of inherited capital as it is the proper utilization of education. The educational establishment has produced the managers—in industry, in the universities, indeed in the Pentagon. Has this education been successful in preparing these men to meet our contemporary challenge?

Let me take a few random examples:

(1) Consider the position of Pope Paul and conservative Catholic authorities on birth control in the face of

our population problems, qualitative and quantitative. Can we say that religious leadership really leads here?

(2) Consider the modern business corporation and its leadership. Has it demonstrated its effectiveness as the agency for the allocation of our rapidly increasing GNP (expected to be $7,300 per capita for a population of 318 million in the year 2000, or $2,321 billion)? Is the present system of investment, production, promotion and sales adequate to making the optimum humane use of our expanding productive capacity? By what values will future allocation be governed? What values do the managerial elite bring to bear on this task?

(3) Consider the State and Defense Departments as the authors and executors of our relationships with the Communist powers and the third world. Do we find here any trace of the beginning of a transcendence of the system of nation-states and super-powers, or even a genuine surpassing of the specific ideologies of the 1930's and 1950's? Does this look at things give us confidence that our enormous destructive capability is in safe hands controlled by wise heads?

(4) Consider the university as the agency for the conservation and creation of values. Do not the universities of this country seem headed for tighter integration into the industry-education-government combine rather than showing signs of becoming a responsible network of independent thinking institutions? Does one see in the functioning of our educational establishment much awareness of the need for the kind of knowledge requisite for determining our future and the wisdom necessary for survival?

(5) Consider the medical profession and the immense technological capacity to be placed in its hands in the

immediate future. Is the self-interest and ideological bigotry displayed by AMA in combating Medicare diagnostic of the spiritual condition of the profession as a whole? Who will become the custodian of the medical welfare of the community in the period to come? The sophisticated have long known that science today becomes a game to be played in a highly competitive arena for high stakes, material and psychological. We have seen this aspect of scientific endeavor surface briefly in the recent rash of heart transplants. Where are ethical restraints to come from?

(6) Consider the space program. What is one to make of the spectacle of our race for space—partly a scientific game, partly a military one? I do not know whether or not Loren Eisely is right when he suggests that the space program is an exercise in futility comparable to the construction of the pyramids in ancient Egypt. But the priority given to space at present in the face of the proportions of our earth-bound problems reminds one of the statement of Henry David Thoreau, who found the most amazing thing about the pyramids the fact that the populace was stupid enough to build them.

In any of these spheres—and we could present many more—can we say that religion has given those most immediately involved a sense of relation, of meaning and of direction to aid them in facing up to their problems? Have the humanistic studies made the practitioners in any of these fields visibly more humane?

Observers of different sorts see various possibilities in these situations. Zbigniew Brzezinski of Columbia University, and recently of the State Department Policy Planning Staff, tends to take an optimistic attitude. He makes on the whole a positive prognosis of the development of what he calls our "technotronic society" based upon technology and especially electronics, and for the "meritocratic democracy" he sees or at least hopes will be developed upon that base. Yet he cannot completely close his eyes to certain problems:

There is a danger in all this, however, that ought not to be neglected. Intense involvement in applied knowledge could gradually prompt a waning of the tradition of learning for the sake of learning. The intellectual community, including the university, could become another "industry," meeting social needs as the market dictates, with intellectuals reaching for the highest material and political rewards. Concern with power, prestige, and the good life could mean an end to the aristocratic ideal of intellectual detachment and the disinterested search for truth.[4]

Joseph Wood Krutch, surveying the literature predicting the year 2000, comes out on the pessimistic side. He believes that the predictors may be looking at the wrong things, at trends rather than ideas and values, and that "the quality of life in the year 2000 may depend as much upon such beliefs, attitudes, and faiths as it does upon the trends recognized by most of the prophets."[5] W. H. Ferry, who is much more concerned with technology and its consequences than with religion, nevertheless sees the problem as fundamentally a religious one. In a highly critical article advocating the regulation of technology, Ferry identifies the basic religious crisis underlying our present technological dilemmas. He suggests that the American "infatuation" with technology as "ultimately the medicine for all ills" may be our basic problem. "Technology is the American theology, promising salvation by material works."[6] Let us add that technology performs this function because no other substitute has successfully tackled the problems involved. Technology could usurp the place of theology (and of philosophy) because these fields had themselves long since abdicated. Theology has indeed begun again to face the modern dilemma with intelligence and authenticity of concern, but it has not been able to overcome the deep religious crisis of our age, the dimensions of which I tried to depict in the first chapter.[7]

To this analysis should be added the words of another sociologist of religion, Peter L. Berger, as reported in the *New York Times*. "By the 21st century, religious believers are likely to be found only in small sects, huddled together to resist a worldwide secular culture." Berger suggests that the churches will become "cognitive minorities" in the period ahead and will experience massive pressures to conform with the secular culture in which they will find themselves. "The traditional religions are likely to survive in small enclaves and pockets and perhaps there will be enclaves of Asian religion in America too." This is the learned and considered opinion of a man who himself believes that "the decline of religion has nothing to do with its truth or falsity." Berger suggests that religion may be approaching "the stage of self-liquidation"—a stage he believes Protestantism has already reached.[8]

THE HISTORICAL BACKGROUND OF THE
CONTEMPORARY CRISIS

In order to better understand the import of the statement made earlier that Christianity, humanism and science, the three basic components of the Western Culture, contained elements of false consciousness, let us look briefly at the historical background of each.[9]

Christianity, arising in Palestine in those historical experiences which lay behind the New Testament scriptures, was by the year 200 transformed into the hierarchically organized sacramental church. The expectations of *parousia* were replaced by an emphasis upon the present. A here-and-now relation to God through Christ in the sacraments became central. The church as the institution founded by Christ was seen to be the agency of God's redemptive work. An earlier chiliastic indifference to the world affected by the specific temper of declining antique culture was transformed into a contempt for the world. Although the church fought the Gnostic religions of alienation and maintained its Hebraic creationist theology, it became decidedly otherworldly in its values as we have already seen. The difficult conditions of life at the time were conducive to the development of these tendencies.

Yet the church did accept much of classical culture, and as one consequence the highly organized ecclesiastical organization came to have as its ideational counterpart an elaborate theology which defined man's meaning, his ontological situation and moral condition, in considerable detail. This vast organizational-liturgical-intellectual complex became central to medieval society and served as the guardian of man's inner life—the keeper of his conscience and indeed of his total consciousness. Yet the church also transmitted the thought of the Greeks—transmitted and rediscovered it—and in that lay the seeds of the later development of humanism and science. When the propitious social conditions were achieved, these embryonic elements would begin their development.

The establishment of civil government in the 10th and 11th centuries, the development of trade and towns in the 11th and afterwards, the founding of the universities in the 13th, the extension of commerce in the 14th and 15th —all these provided the conditions necessary for the new humanism and the new science. Yet while Greek was lost in the West, Latin was retained in the face of the vernacular developments of the 6th to the 9th century. Consequently the West never completely lost touch with ancient culture. By the 11th and 12th centuries the works of writers like Horace, Persius, Juvenal and Terence were well-known among the literate. In the 12th century Plato's *Timaeus* was available (in the partial translation of Calcidiis together with the translator's commentary), as were several versions of the first two treatises of Aristotle's *Organon* translated from the Arabic. The medieval church proposed to the men of that age—to the clergy and laity, both with minor modifications—the model of Christian life developed by the monasteries, which were the loci of spiritual and cultural development in the earlier period.

With the rise of town life, however, the possibilities of a development of humanism came more and more to be realized. It represented the first beginnings in a breakthrough of the otherworldly outlook which the church had long taught. Humanism, however, was to be affected not only by the success of city life but also by the difficult problems that beseiged the church in the Middle Ages, by that time an old institution rigidly structured in its organization and its ideas, and also by the conflicts and chaos characteristic of the development of the dynastic states and city states against the Empire. Humanism came to embody both elements of optimism and of pessimism and an ambiguous set of attitudes toward the church and otherworldly religion.

The variety of conflicting tendencies characteristic of developing humanism is to be seen early in the life and writings of Francesco Petrarch (1304–1374). He combined a Latin scholarship with an enthusiasm for the new vernacular. He possessed both an enthusiasm for the Roman past and an attitude that anticipated the Italian future. He was indeed a Christian and experienced a kind of Augustinian religious experience, but he attempted to put it together with the classical spirit of Cicero. He realized and affirmed the beauty of women, of the world, and of the classics and at the same time repented much of it in the typical Christian mode, speaking of his failures and vanities. He saw the world not simply as the place of sin and suffering, although he considered his age a degenerate one, but the world was also a place of spiritual value.

Petrarch was, in his own words, a Christian as Cicero would have been a Christian had he known Christ. In 1342 he wrote his *Secretum* after his brother became a monk of the Carthusian order. It was a kind of justification of his own for not doing the same thing. In it he composed imaginary dialogues with St. Augustine, in which the great saint admonishes him to consider death, to concern himself with his soul's welfare and to renounce the vain things of this life. In response, Petrarch confesses his weaknesses but he does not repudiate the world. He is aware of life's misery and its transience, but he also sees its this-worldly goodness, and he seeks a balance—a Christian classical balance. As to the institutional church, he was critical. He considered Aristotelianism a misfortune, although in his own literary way he affirmed, as did

Thomas, that the effort to perfect nature could be a path
to God. He opposed the Latin Averroists and defended
humanism against their brand of natural scientism. He
supported with enthusiasm the Roman Republic of Reinzo
in 1347.[10]

The rise of urban life and the rise of humanism ushered
in a new epoch for Europe. The world of the past was
recovered—a process that began early in the Middle Ages
—and a new world of the future was simultaneously
opened up. Within religion itself heretical tendencies had
long since made their appearance as new ideas threatened
the rigid closure of the church's teachings. The synthesis
of Greek science and Christian teaching achieved by
Aquinas did not last and never became the dominant
outlook of the schools. Now a host of old ideas were rein-
troduced. Cardinal Bassarion, Cosimo de' Medici, Marsilio
Ficino, Pico della Mirandola and on to the burning of
Giordano Bruno—all symbolize aspects of this many-sided
development. The Renaissance sought a return to the
past and at the same time an affirmation of life in the
world. It was clear to many that something could be done
to alter the world. The humanists' concern with texts
introduced Western men to a kind of criticism which
would greatly affect their thinking in the future. Moreover, this combination of recognizing the world as alter-
able with the critical recognition that earlier epochs had
different views and premises than those of their own
period gave the men of that age a sense of history lacking
in the Middle Ages.

Humanism was both a counter movement to Christianity and a movement within Christianity to reconcile
it to the restored culture of antiquity. Humanists in some
cases rejected some aspects of the church, as can be seen

in Valla's opposition to monastic vows as denigrating nature, the widespread humanist antagonism to scholasticism and the support often given by humanists to secular rulers against the church. Yet most were Christian, and some tried to make use of classical knowledge to reform the church. Among the Catholics, Erasmus and More may be suggested as examples. Despite the marked anti-Renaissance character of important aspects of the Reformation, there were among the Protestants, from Melanchthon on, many humanistic scholars. Among the Calvinists the influence of Peter Ramus, who was concerned with methodology and systematization, was clearly evident. To all these developments, at the end of the 15th century exploration and discovery added another "new world." But that brings us to our third component—science. Political ambition, religious aspiration and economic drives spurred discovery, but geographical science stood at the center of its successes. Before Henry the Navigator, the Portuguese had long pursued and supported such studies.

Our own epoch and our civilization became in many ways a new world, and what is most characteristic of that new world is science. The emergence of modern science in the 17th century represents a tremendous change in human thinking to which nothing in history can compare, not excluding the conversion of Europe to Christianity. Much has been written concerning the relation of science to the basic premises of our traditional thinking, the fundamental assumptions of Western man's view of the world and his attitude toward it which Christianity had introduced and nurtured in the West. It was a view that the world was an orderly world created by a rational God and knowable to man made in God's image, and that man had been told by God to subdue the earth and to name its creatures. The acceptance of Greek rationality by the early church and the cultivation of rigorous philosophical thinking in the medieval university disciplined the Western mind and prepared it for scientific development.

Science had originally been invented by the Greeks not because they were the first to observe and study nature but because they sought the intelligible, unchanging and permanent "something" behind all the flux of observation and tried to formulate it in abstract theory. In the Hellenic setting, however, science was only secondarily related to those practical matters and that practical attitude of mind that might have stimulated it to continual development. In other places, as at Babylon, although much knowledge of astronomy and other matters was gained such activity did not lead to a demythologization of thought. In Greece, science began in a society of which slavery was an important institution and which regarded the work of the craftsman as servile and banal. This was not the whole picture to be sure, as may be seen in the medical writings from Hippocrates to Galen, the engineering equipment attributed to Archimedes, the writings of Ctesibus, Appolodorus, Hero, Vitruvius, Cato, Varro and others. From these ancient sources, supplemented by the works of transition figures like Isidore and Bede, some of ancient science came into the Middle Ages, but from the 5th to the 10th century a great deal of scientific and technical as well as humanistic knowledge was lost. From the latter century onwards, however, Europe advanced in scientific knowledge and in the effective utilization of technique. In the Middle Ages the older separation of men of learning from men who did the work was further broken down, and scholars became concerned with the practical uses of knowledge. Before the year 1500 technology in agriculture, milling and manufacturing had made great strides.

The urban life of the late Middle Ages and the Renaissance was conducive to the development of science. The Renaissance represented the climax of that long process of rediscovering and assimilating the culture of antiquity that had begun in the Carolingian period—in law, in letters, in philosophy and in science. Modern science as it developed in the 17th century stood both as inheritor and continuator of medieval scholasticism and as its antagonist as well. It was also a part of that turn to things of this world which humanism represented, but it was at the same time partly in conflict with the humanist cast of mind. What happened in the 17th century has been justifiably called "the scientific revolution." It was the climax of a long development, and it rested upon the philosophical, scientific and technological attainments of the past—behind Newton was Galileo, behind Galileo, Buridan and Nicholas of Oresme; behind Harvey stood Padua.

But the scientific revolution of the 17th century represented something new—a vast shift in the way men saw their world and in the way they set about systematically coping with that world. "It was not simply a continuation of the increasing attention to observation and to the experimental and mathematical methods that had been going on since the 13th century, because the change took on an altogether new speed and a quality that made it dominate European thinking."[11] It was a shift in thinking that was not simply the result of new data and which ran far in advance of the invention of the necessary instruments in every realm. It was a shift that placed emphasis upon experiment and mathematics and in an important sense "geometrized" abstract thought. It completely changed the way men looked at nature and at the world. This was true to such an extent that in a few decades the Aristotelian world of the scholastics and the Neoplatonic world of the humanists appeared as simply quaint to men of science.

Herbert Butterfield has declared that the scientific revolution of the 17th century "represents one of the great episodes in human experience." His characterization is worth quoting:

> It represents one of those periods when new things are brought into the world and into history out of men's own creative ability, and their own wrestlings with truth. There does not seem to be any sign that the ancient world, before its heritage had been dispersed, was moving toward anything like the scientific revolution, or that the Byzantine Empire, in spite of the continuity of its classical tradition, would ever have taken hold of ancient thought and so remoulded it by a great transforming power . . . And not only was a new factor introduced into history at this time among other factors, but it proved to be so capable of growth, and so many-sided in its operations, that it consciously assumed a directing role from the very first, and, so to speak, began to take control of the other factors—just as Christianity in the middle ages had come to preside over everything else, percolating into every corner of life and thought.[12]

Modern science as a mode of thought possessed two characteristics which enabled it to unlock the hidden knowledge of natural processes at a tremendous rate—mathematical abstraction, which cut through the complexities of lived experience and simplified it, and the power of generalization which mathematics entailed. It was, as we saw in chapter one, precisely these qualities which enabled science to become such a tremendous force for demythologization of thought, since all forms of thought not subsumable under the formulations of abstract science tended to become *mythos* for those strategic thinkers who were most closely related to and affected by science, such as Descartes, Hobbes and Locke. After Newton the *"philosophes"* popularized much of this kind of thinking among the bourgeoisie.

It is true that these are not the only demythologizing elements in modern science. The theory of evolution in the 19th century in the non-mathematized field of biology upset traditional religion in another way. But science derives much of its acid solvent power vis-a-vis tradition and much of its capacity for dynamic growth from these two characteristics. They place science in sharp contrast to the basically static ideals proposed by Christianity and humanism. Science came into existence as a part of traditional religious culture and as part of emerging humanism; it developed into their most formidable opponent. Today, allied with technology and central to our complex society, it represents an autonomous factor affecting our lives. Is there any wonder under such circumstances that, in W. H. Ferry's words, technology should become the theology of contemporary American society.

Christianity dominated the society of the Middle Ages and the church was its institutional embodiment. It directed men to prepare themselves for the life to come and worked out a detailed overall doctrine which it taught its adherents. Humanism came to be a dominant influence upon the intellectuals and some of the rising townsmen of the Renaissance. It rediscovered a new value in this world and directed men's attention to it. Science came into existence in the soil prepared by Christianity and humanism but is also in conflict with both. From the emergence of modern science at the end of the 17th century it soon came, in Crombie's words, "to dominate European thinking," in Butterfield's, "to take control of the other factors—just as Christianity in the middle ages had come to preside over everything else, percolating into every corner of life and thought."

The institutional embodiment of this science in our day is not simply the scientific disciplines in the university—that would be a short-sighted and most naive suggestion. It is the total industry-government-education complex. In this setting our science and technology take on a kind of autonomy irrespective of their real relevance to the needs of modern man, just as Christianity in the Middle Ages took on such an autonomy when often it failed to be relevant to the real activities and needs of the men of that time. Or like medieval Christianity, science and technology often come to serve the dominant interests of established elites. Science and technology are important conquests of the human mind. They are indeed the glory of our age as was Christianity the glory of the Middle Ages, but like Christianity in that period they are one-sided and without qualification and guidance can lead us all to destruction.

Religion and the humanities experience their own crises because they have not been able to render themselves genuinely relevant to life in contemporary society. They have been forced to live in the world created by science and industry. Science, as we have seen, contributed elements to human thinking which tended to dissolve the basic notions of religious thought as myth in the pejorative sense of that word and to reduce the rich content of lived experience as apprehended in the humanities to a "subjective" concern and a matter of secondary and derived characteristics. Many years ago Andrew Dickson White wrote a two-volume work concerned with what he called the "warfare between science and theology." His fundamental allegation was the reactionary character of Christian theology which opposed the development of both science and capitalism, which White felt provided the basis for a free secular civilization. Whatever one may think of White's value biases, he saw one thing clearly— what science did to demythologize man's world view, capitalism did to disenchant the world of experience. Marx summed it up in the observation we noted in the previous chapter: "The bourgeoisie, wherever it has got the upper hand, has put an end to all feudal, patriarchal, idyllic relations. It has pitilessly torn asunder the motley feudal ties that bound man to his 'natural superiors,' and has left no other ties between man and man than naked self-interest, than callous 'cash payment.'"[13]

Until the 19th century, the market economy was by and large subjected to noneconomic rules and regulations based upon traditional social values. This is not to say that such regulations necessarily embodied social justice, but that they did represent the recognition that noneconomic considerations were necessary in the distribution of economic goods. It was after about 1780 in the West that the market economy began to free itself entirely from such restraints. From the end of the 19th century to our day we have found it necessary to recreate social regulation and politically structured redistribution to supplement and correct the working of the market. The free market lasted but a brief while in the Western world and hardly existed at all elsewhere. In view of this it is amazing how much it has become an ideological element in the make-up of American conservatism! The freeing of economic activity from social restraints was of course resisted by the church which was long suspicious of money-making as perilous to the soul and which saw economic activity as a means to life and not an autonomous activity for the enrichment of elites. Money from its first introduction into the ancient world has always acted as a solvent of traditional reciprocities and as a liberator of individualist ambitions. This can be seen from the writings of Hesiod to the sermons of the preachers of the late Middle Ages and the Reformation.

As the commercial revolution began in the Middle Ages and continued into the 18th century, centers of economic life arose which exhibited the capitalist spirit. Not simply among the Calvinists, as Weber showed, but also in Venice and Florence, in Germany and Flanders the new spirit flourished. By the time Adam Smith wrote *The Wealth of Nations* in 1776 even the English countryside had become enmeshed in the developing commercial society. National markets had been developing in Western Europe since the middle of the 18th century, the price of grain became national not local, and large scale use of money came to be a fact even in the rural areas.

Thus economic life disenchanted the world and helped to make the world of Christianity less credible. The bourgeois lived in a new world. Writing of the year 1772 in France, Bernard Groethuysen said, "The bourgeois had been confident of his own strength and had become master of the world." He continued: "The great and the poor, the former to justify their rank and wealth, the latter to console themselves for having none, turned to the church and rendered it homage; but what reason had the bourgeois for doing likewise? A child of this world, he had grown up without the assistance of the Church. The God of the Christians had never wanted to recognize him; what he was, he owed to himself; he had appointed himself his own providence, and was not prepared to recognize any other."[14] Economic development had secularized much of daily life and had pushed religion gradually but steadily from the center to the sidelines. Concluded R. H. Tawney:

When the age of the Reformation begins, economics is still a branch of ethics, and ethics of theology; all human activities are treated as falling within a single scheme, whose character is determined by the spiritual destiny of mankind; the appeal of theorists is to natural law, not to utility; the legitimacy of economic transactions is tried by reference less to movements in the market than to moral standards derived from the traditional teaching of the Christian Church; the Church is regarded as a society wielding theoretical, and sometimes practical, authority in social affairs. The secularization of political thought, which was to be the work of the next two centuries, had profound reactions on social speculation, and by the Restoration the whole perspective, at least in England, had been revolutionized. Religion has been converted from the keystone which holds together the social edifice into one department within it, and the idea of a rule of right is replaced by economic expediency as the arbiter of policy and the criterion of conduct.[15]

THE CONTEMPORARY CRISIS: WHAT CAN BE DONE?

What can be done about our contemporary historical predicament is not a question that any one of us can answer, but one rather to which we must all strive to provide tentative and suggestive answers. The churches and the educational institutions are in need of a continual self-examination; for them as for the rest of us the Socratic dictum is more true than ever that the unexamined life is not fit for human beings. They already have some sense of this and they have already begun. Here on the record one suspects that the churches have gone farther than have educational institutions. The post-conciliar turmoil within the Roman Catholic Church is most interesting in this regard, and indeed it is entirely possible that the ultimate fate of Christianity may depend upon the outcome of the next few decades of Catholic attempts at *aggiornamento*.[16] How shall educational institutions go about their self-examination? What is the chief problem facing them? What is the end-result of this analysis?

Christianity emphasized personal transcendence in relation to a transcendent God and a sphere of spirit *(pneuma)* to which man could rise and in which he could find an ultimate relationship with Being. But Christianity put forward this insight embodied in otherworldly doctrines which took man's attention away from the tasks facing him in this world. We have already pointed out that it is one of the great ironies of our history that Western man achieved the most impressive this-worldly accomplishments although his fundamental world view gave him little basis for significant interpretation of his achievements. Although Christian doctrine held that being was good and asserted the reality of history in relation to its own central teaching, the otherworldly teachings of the church in effect gave men a pessimistic view of being here below and tended to derogate the events of secular history to a position of minor importance except where they threatened the concerns of faith or the institutional interests of the church.

Humanism affirmed the world, its beauty and its capacity for goodness, and emphasized the this-worldly vocation of man as a creator and appreciator of culture and as the agent of his own self-realization. It did this for long within the Christian framework but eventually outside it and in rebellion against it. As the church possessing the sense of transcendence asked significant ontological and ethical questions about man's existence and destiny, so humanism called men's attention to other dimensions of human existence than those ethical and religious dimensions stressed by the church, and made man aware of his own many-sided complexity. Moreover, where the church stressed the reality of sin and the danger of pride *(hybris)*, humanism stressed the complementary recognition of man's capacity for good and his right to self-confidence. Where the church was one-sided in the interpretation which it gave its own doctrines, and by its underemphasizing the spiritual significance of man's endeavors in this world gave a partialness to the Christian outlook, so too the humanists, seeing man's potential for self-cultivation, creation and aesthetic participation in a literary and aristocratic mode, often imparted to the viewpoint of the humanities a partial perspective which made it difficult to relate their insights to the lives of ordinary men. To emphasize cultivation of man's potential without reference to transcendence, as humanism came to do, is to foreshorten man's view of himself and his condition; to do so without the means for democratizing opportunity put at our disposal by science is to restrict fulfillment to a fortunate few and thereby make one's humanism less than fully humane.

Science saw man as a cognitive and manipulating being —("master and possessor of nature," Descartes; "reading the language in which God wrote creation," Galileo; "knowledge is power," Bacon)—utilizing abstract mathematical thought to gain a fantastic leverage over his situation. But at the same time it tended to consign all experiences not translatable into its own type of conceptualization to a limbo of epiphenomena, and all relationships to man, nature and the Beyond other than the narrowly cognitive and abstract to the sphere of subjectivity.[17] Hence a total view of man was foreshortened and the human situation only partially apprehended. (For example, it was a struggle to reintroduce the element of understanding the point of view of the people being studied—*verstehen*—back into sociology.)[18] To seek the material mastery of the human situation without concern for the interior growth of man and the requirements of human community among men, as "scientism" and especially scientism in alliance with industry attempted to do, was to permit the means to displace the ends and to become ourselves the victims of our own superlative material powers.

Is it not the basic challenge to learning in our day to overcome the elements of partialness, foreshortening, truncation of man and his situation, and false-consciousness in these three major components of our culture? Is it not here above all that the times call for criticism and creativity? We must learn how to confront the genuine contributions of each to our better understanding of our total situation and make their insights available to ourselves for our self-understanding in our present historical situation. Do we not now begin to see the vague outlines of what education ought to be—the effort toward understanding man from his history and his works and the cultivation of men capable of humanizing themselves and the society of men on earth? With this vision it becomes clear that the integration of education into the industry-government-education combine tends to lead us in another direction. It tends to make higher education a logistical resource providing the "trained people" to perform the requisite tasks of the vast superstructure of the industry-government-business complex; it becomes the training ground for *apparatchiki*. Practical tasks must be done and people must be trained to do them, but expediency is not policy nor is training education. I do not say that education today has succumbed to this danger. Rather it is torn apart by a number of confusing tendencies among which this particular one is quite prominent.

The great sociological question arises: who sets the goals and proposes the tasks for this huge industry-government-education complex which is the central institutional structure of our society? There is indeed a way in which it is fair to say that they set themselves; they are derived from the situational exigencies which face numberless decision-makers in the system who make penultimate (and indeed quite antepenultimate) decisions about "practical matters." Overall goals when stated at all—as when President Eisenhower had a commission state goals for Americans—never turn out under present conditions to be expressible in an idiom which relates them to this level of effective decision-making and hence tend to remain platitudes. We simply do not yet understand enough about this new society in which we live and which we have evolved in our ideological semi-consciousness to know how to make such statements meaningfully.

It is necessary here for us to take a number of other

aspects of this situation into account. Ideational systems do not provide their own motivation. The role of ideas is rather to define the situation and thereby provide a context for action. In that way ideas affect action and its consequences. Yet ideas affect action in other ways as well. Most significantly, they evoke deeper levels of human motives and canalize human energies along their own ideationally defined pathways. Christianity, humanism and science appealed to men—called to them, struck cords in the human makeup far deeper than cognition or practicality. They have each elicited a great variety of motivation throughout our history. Religion has elicited motives ranging from the purest effort after communion with transcendence to the narrowest and most brutal national, class, and individual interests. Humanism also has canalized a multitude of motivations behind its aims and activities, ranging from aggression and aggrandizement to the purest aesthetic and spiritual expression. Science has not only evoked man's curiosity, disciplined it and directed it, but also has called forth fiercely competitive motives and indeed has often become the expression of a sizable component of aggression.

Human actions are the expression of a great variety of coincidental motives and this is as true in religion, humanistic studies and science as elsewhere. Therefore it follows that in trying to understand the complicated inter-relations of these three and their relation to the daily lives of men, we must understand something of what they mean for men in concrete human activity. We must be aware of the level of interest in human behavior. As Groethuysen said in the quotation above, the rich and the powerful in the late 18th century embraced the church in order to defend their rank and wealth, the poor to console themselves for the lack of either. The bourgeois rejected it because he found its teaching and itself as a community incompatible with the identity he had evolved in his own autonomous activity in the business world. Our understanding will never be genuinely helpful until we can take account of this level of human behavior. We must understand the way in which people take spiritual postures which will provide satisfactory lifestances for them in their concretely experienced situations.

This complex relation of motive to meaning is not to be understood in terms of individuals alone. Man is indeed a social animal, and his interests, his postures, his aspirations and his affinity for ideas are all related to his relationship to his fellows. Nations, ethnic groups, classes, strata—all of these present a level of interest related to the individual and group defense of or achievement of what we have now come to call identity—a self-hood and a membership in a community. Let us look at a brief historical illustration. When Galileo wrote his famous *Dialogue* the evidence for the heliocentric hypothesis was quite ambiguous, and indeed Galileo did not argue uniformly well on all points. Tycho Brahe, the greatest empirical astronomer the world had yet seen, could not go along with it without serious—very serious—modification. In the face of this ambiguous situation men formed into two hostile camps. The churchmen took the conservative side. It is not too difficult to understand why they did so. They felt the new hypothesis would undermine religious faith. They as churchmen were the protectors of faith, and faith indeed provided them with their own *raison d'être*. They had both psychological and material interests which inclined them strongly to the negative. But what about the men who took the affirmative? The cognitive reasons were not objectively convincing; what motivational factors threw the balance toward Galileo's view? There must have been a number of such motives, ranging from the preference for the improved mathematical elegance of the new theory to a desire to aggress the ecclesiastical establishment with its rigid intellectual structures.

In America, where higher education has long been the arena in which the traditions of the home faced the world of the Enlightenment, such complexities of motivation have indeed long been at work. Our educational system has long been the locus of a process of emancipation of youth from the traditions of their fathers—fathers of the rural Middle West, or the Bible Belt, or the Irish, Italian or Slavic village, the Jewish Shtetl, and a host of others. We have hidden it from ourselves behind a formal vocabulary which saw man as an abstraction rather than an historically specific being. In our educational system there are at work complex configurations of motives not unlike the kind we saw in the Galileo case. They are part of the picture of assimilation and success in America and they involve the deepest levels of emerging personal and group identity.[19]

If the educational system is where the identity of Americans begins to be shaped, the occupational structure is where it comes to whatever fulfillment it does in fact achieve. That means that within the industry-government-education structure men pursue a number of goals; they project their own needs for expression and formation, for protection and security, their needs for selfhood, into the aims and goals of organization. A combination of ascribed identity elements—religious, ethnic, social and economic —together with achieved ones—professional status, organ-

izational power and position, reputation—influence and
affect the behavior of Americans as they act out the drama
of their lives within the complex structures of this technologically advanced society.

We have suggested that what is needed is a many-sided
understanding of man based upon his history and his
works. Our education must pursue this goal in depth;
it must learn to take account of the deeper wellsprings
of human action and their relation to the events of our
history and our contemporary life. In this task the study
of history and of the humanities stand in the forefront.
But the social sciences have a most important role. If we
are to understand man and his works, if we are to catch
a glimpse of the kind of dramas men act out in this world
and the elements of human aspiration that go into them
as well as the difficulties which they seek to surmount,
then we must put our sociology and psychology together
in an effort to create social sciences in depth. We need to
learn how to find out and how to understand what is
actually going on in the social structures and processes in
which we are enmeshed. We must create a *realsociologie*
which will enable us to identify and understand the historically specific processes going on in our own time.
Only through such understanding can freedom be enhanced and human welfare authentically promoted.

Hegel thought—in that more optimistic age—that ideas
were always successful in enlisting human drives, passions,
and motivations in the thrust of human freedom. He
spoke of the "cunning of reason" which enabled the can-
alization of even the most reprehensible motives behind
the enhancement of freedom itself. We can no longer feel
this confidence. The record to date of our bloody century
indicates that the cunning of reason is indeed problema-

tical. While ideas have at times canalized human efforts in the direction of the further humanization of man and his community, they have also been exploited as screens to hide—even from the actors themselves—baser motives which have led to destruction. Reason in Hegel's sense has often been debased into rationalization in Freud's. Such debasing of reason must be unmasked by knowledge. Freud has shown that despite rationalization, reason can indeed untangle the skein of motivation and self-deception and enlarge its sphere of influence. This is true in individual life but it is no less true in the life of communities. The cunning of reason can only be made a fact of history by reason itself.

The university is reason's smithy; it is the place where man's capacity to free himself of his past and to assume responsibility for his future must be forged and hammered out. There at least the process must begin. But this will require a real understanding of our situation. It will mean the cutting through of vested interests; it will require a combination of reason and good faith which will enable us to break down the narrow interest-laden partiality of our various positions. It must bring about the kind of intellectual and personal confrontations which will lead toward what Karl Mannheim called a synthesis of perspectives. "Saving knowledge" is no longer a slogan of the eschatological imagination to be sought after by the religious enthusiast and scorned by the educated organization man. It is what we need and must find. But it must be genuine knowledge, tried and tested by reason itself if it indeed is to save us. This need becomes particularly acute for our youthful generations—a consideration with which we shall deal in the next two chapters.

FOOTNOTES

1. Anthony J. Wiener and Herman Kahn, *The Year 2000* (New York: Macmillan, 1967).

2. Bernard Barber, *Drugs and Society* (New York: Russell Sage, 1967).

3. William Clancy, John Cogley, Arthur A. Cohen, Robert Gordis, William Gorman, F. Ernest Johnson, Robert LeKachman, William Lee Miller, *Religion and American Society* (Santa Barbara, California, 1961).

4. Zbigniew Brzezinski, "The American Transition," *The New Republic*, December 23, 1967, p. 21 and *passim*.

5. Joseph Wood Krutch, "What the Year 2000 Won't Be Like," *Saturday Review*, January 20, 1968, p. 14.

6. Wilbur H. Ferry, "Must We Rewrite the Constitution to Control Technology," *Saturday Review*, March 2, 1968, p. 50.

7. See especially the section, "The Religious Crisis; Its Contemporary Urgency."

8. *New York Times*, Sunday, February 25, 1968.

9. I have limited this discussion of religion to Christianity which has been the dominant faith of the West. What is said would be equally true of Judaism. The other-worldly spirit is characteristic of Jewish religion and becomes particularly dominant in Jewish life in times of threat and danger. Jewish "exile" was at its deepest level "cosmic" exile, and the Jew was never at home in this world. This attitude is reflected in the words of the Jewish martyr of the Crusades, the victim of accompanying anti-semitic outbreaks: "For the time being the enemy will slay us . . . and yet we shall live and flourish, our souls will be in Paradise [reflected] in the great shining mirror for ever and ever . . . Above all, do not question the justice of the Holy One, Blessed Be He, and Blessed Be His Name . . . Happy shall we be if we do His will, and happy everyone who is slain and slaughtered and dies for the Sanctification of His Name. Such a one is destined for the world to come." F. Y. Baer, "The Religious-Social Tendency of *Sefer Hasidim*" (Hebrew), *Zion*, III, 1938, pp. 15–17. Quoted from Jacob Katz, *Exclusiveness and Tolerance* (New York: Oxford, 1961), p. 86. I am not suggesting

that Christians and Jews did not face and cope with this world; it is clear that they did. I am pointing out that their religious point of view gave no adequate basis for interpreting their this-worldly experience and thus understanding its relevant human significance for them and their communities.

10. See E. H. Wilkins, *The Life of Petrarch* (Chicago: Chicago University Press, 1961).

11. A. C. Crombie, *Medieval and Early Modern Science,* Vol. II, (Garden City, New York: Doubleday, 1959), p. 122.

12. Herbert Butterfield, *The Origins of Modern Science* (New York: Macmillan, 1951), pp. 139–140.

13. Karl Marx, "The Communist Manifesto," quoted from *Handbook of Marxism,* E. Burns (ed.).

14. Bernard Groethuysen, *The Bourgeois: Catholicism vs Capitalism in 18th Century France,* M. Ilford, tr. (New York: Holt, 1968).

15. R. H. Tawney, *Religion and the Rise of Capitalism* (New York: New American Library, 1949), p. 288.

16. See Thomas F. O'Dea, *The Catholic Crisis* (Boston, Massachusetts: Beacon Press, 1968).

17. For example see E. A. Burtt, *The Metaphysical Foundations of Modern Physical Science,* 2nd rev. ed. (New York: Humanities, 1954).

18. See for example Talcott Parsons, *The Structure of Social Action* (Glencoe, Illinois: Macmillan (Free Press), 1949).

19. See, as an admirable effort to develop a realistic sociology in this respect, Milton M. Gordon, *Assimilation in American Life* (New York: Oxford, 1964).

IV

Youth
and the Search for Meaning

American young people are making a varied and somewhat confusing response to the world of the mid 1960s.
In Vietnam, a sizeable number of them, drawn disproportionately from disadvantaged and deprived strata of the
population, are giving an impressive example of courage
and intelligence. It has indeed been suggested that our
military units in Vietnam represent the best fighting
force this country has put in the field in all of its wars,
that they constitute a highly competent army, and that
their morale is remarkably good. These evaluations are
all the more striking because the war in which these men
are engaged is an extremely difficult one and is being
fought under military and political conditions which
could well prove demoralizing for men in combat. They
are striking also because of the young age of the soldiers
and marines involved. Melville said that all wars are
boyish, but this one is especially so—and on both sides.
American journalists looking at these young men under
combat conditions have asked how our affluent society has
managed to produce them.

At home in the States, the more literate and more edu-

cated of our youth show signs of deep malaise and dissatis-
faction. Demonstrations have become common on the
campus, and college youth protest our engagement in the
Vietnamese war and identify themselves with the cause
of civil rights and with the victims of hard core poverty
in a prosperous society. That there is "unrest" among
college and university youth is clearly the case. There are
the demonstrations of advocacy and protest; some seek
outlets for their unsatisfied yearnings and aspirations in
a "cult of experience," or even by embracing the "absurd."
Psychedelic drugs, the "Beat" posture, and a dramatizing
of absurdity are taken up as the answer to a total situation
felt to be absurd in an almost ultimate sense. Others turn
to "people and service-oriented" experiences and careers
in the Peace Corps, in the churches, in private organizations. These protesting and seceding youth would appear
to be disproportionately from the more affluent and
established strata of society.

The palpable evidence suggests that the upper and
lower strata of American youth tend to experience today's
world differently. We do not have facts and figures to
give us an accurate picture of the distribution of such
responses among the young. We do know that people
under twenty-five years of age make up over half of our
total population. And we know also that youth seem not
only more numerous (which they are) but more influential than ever before. Advertisers will tell you that the
"teen market" is an affluent and influential reality, and
Time magazine recently made the entire generation its
man of the year. It seems most likely that both the fighting
men in Vietnam—who are in high proportion either
volunteers for military service or volunteers for service in

Vietnam—and the protesting and seceding students on our campuses represent minority attitudes among our youth. We all suspect, I presume, that the majority of American youth, in and out of college, follow the established patterns and walk the well trod paths in jobs and careers and in their personal lives. Yet it seems also that mass higher education and mass media have had their effect and that many, among the more usual, experience to some extent the strains affecting those farther out. The questioning of the "establishment," the "sexual revolution," and some degree of spiritual malaise would seem to be characteristic of large numbers of young people.

Lacking the essential statistical information and knowledge of the facts concerning where the masses of our young people stand, we must confine ourselves here to the general situation. We shall attempt to present a structural analysis of the position of today's youth; suggest how in that position they see the adult world; and why they respond to it as they do. Our general analysis reveals that today young people are more free than ever before: free in terms of societal and familial constraints; free with respect to religious or ideological restrictions; and free in their possession of greater means for pursuing their own aims and acting out their own impulses. It reveals further that adult society confronts youth as a large, objective, and alienated structure which demands that they submit themselves to it and fit themselves into it, and that at the same time its objective functional and moral justifications seem far less secure than in previous times. In this situation the usual responses of youth to the adult world— reluctance to take on the restraints and responsibilities of adulthood, and generational conflict of fathers and sons—are tremendously exacerbated and exaggerated. Let us turn first to the analysis of the position of youth in contemporary American society.

Any society is a matter of established patterns of human behavior deemed right and proper by those involved, or at least by enough of them in strategic places to give the established patterns continuity. These patterns of behavior involve the allocation of power, influence, wealth, and prestige. Societies involve a division of labor and a division of the fruits of labor, a differential distribution of life possibilities and opportunities, an open or covert establishment of a hierarchy of authority and worth. All societies have been and are structured along two axes or dimensions; social relations are either between superior and subordinate—master and apprentice, employer and employee, father and son, age and youth, etc.—or between equals—brothers, citizens, etc. Most societies have placed the overwhelming emphasis upon the vertical dimension, the superior-subordinate axis. But even in the most hierarchical societies we do find egalitarian associations—age groups in traditional Africa, secret societies of traditional China, etc.—and in these the individual finds escape from the pressure of contiguous superiority and supervision into the world of his peers. Yet in most societies the vertical axis, the hierarchical principle, remained the dominant one and "peer group" relations were of functional significance chiefly as "safety valves."

Christianity from the first contained an element of egalitarianism which had great significance throughout

Western history. In the early church there was a stress both on individual and community, but as the ecclesiastical organization developed, the hierarchical emphasis became visibly dominant. The egalitarian inspiration and motif, however, in both religious and secular form, tended to come to the surface at various times, often eventuating in schism and heresy. Political life also remained largely dominated by the hierarchical principle, although throughout the Middle Ages, the rise of the town and the burgher citizen, the freedom of the serfs, and the opportunities of the lowly born to advance in the church all contributed to that long term trend toward equality which Tocqueville called "a great providential drift." When in 1789 the French Revolution proclaimed *Liberté, Egalité, Fraternité,* and enacted the abolition of "feudalities," a new age of Western history began. The marked emphasis of Western social structure would now be increasingly placed upon the horizontal axis or egalitarian dimension.

This change in emphasis in the social structure of the West was related to and accompanied by an analogous change in the Western point of view—the Western mentality. Religion tended to be progressively relegated from the market place and from the council halls, and within religion itself a process of rationalization and demythologization became pronounced. The secular sphere became of central interest with necessary emphasis upon the political and economic activities of the layman, while the world of the sacred became increasingly residual. The ontological mind was replaced more and more by the problem-solving mentality, and worldly concerns assumed centrality, legitimacy, and a capacity to elicit the enthusiasm of men. Science developed and further stripped the

veil of projection from the world, and indeed often de-
nuded men of the capability for aesthetic and religious
relationship. This was a process of the secularization of
culture, but it was also one of human emancipation from
the constraint of orthodoxies and traditions and the self-
limiting effects of myth and superstition. Secularization
emptied out much of the religious substance of the culture of the West. Emancipation freed Western man and
brought him into confrontation with the challenge of
genuine adulthood. This great historic process—seculari-
zation-emancipation—supported the structural shift from
vertical to horizontal dimension in society and weakened,
when it did not totally negate, the sacralization of rank
and authority. A more secular egalitarian society replaced
the former sacral hierarchies; reverence gave way to criticism; ontological justification to functional convenience.

In the 1780s England experienced that socio-economic
process which we now call "take off." The accumulation
of capital and its reinvestment in productive enterprise
achieved the beginning of the process of continuous economic development. The previous rationalization of life
had brought about a great growth in commerce and in
agriculture, but there began in the 1780s that remarkable
transformation known as the Industrial Revolution. From
the beginning of the 19th century the Western world has
experienced an enormous expansion of its productivity
and its capacity to alter and control its environment.
Population increased and was drawn to the cities, and
the Western world became largely urbanized as the decades went by. Industry also made available to the common
man mass-produced articles of use in every department
of life and by and large freed all men from dependence
upon and immersion in the rhythms and processes of

nature as is the case in a traditional peasant society. More-over, industry not only urbanized and put large groups of us together in urban concentrations of population; not only uprooted us from nature and gave us a new man-made environment and new pleasures and needs; it also introduced and developed on a grand scale the notion of segmented and functional authority. Authority at work reflects the removal of the place of work from that of residence. It is limited to a specific sphere of competence with respect to time, place, and the range of behavior to which it is relevant. What developed was a society pro-gressively becoming egalitarian and secular, and one in which men lived under urban conditions removed from nature.

Under these conditions the functions of the family changed radically. The family had in the West long been an important productive unit as well as an affectual one —a unit that supervised many sides of the life and activi-ties of its members. Industrialism and urbanism resulted in a society which more and more took over educative, nurturant, and recreational activities of the family and gave them to other agencies. The curtailment of the family and development of "segmented" and "limited" authority at work, together with the continual shortening of the working day, created greater and greater "free" periods of time in which the individual was under no authority or restraint except those of the distant and largely negative requirements of the Law.

The Industrial Revolution involved a Communications Revolution. Of this ongoing phenomenon two aspects are fundamental: mass media and mass higher education. Both of these created a high degree of psychic mobility in people. They give us the ability to imagine things different from the way they are at present or have been in the past, the capacity to see ourselves in other functions, places and roles, and the capability of designing a totally different plot for the drama of life than that suggested by tradition and precedent. Moreover, scientific technology, the labor movement, and social reform have turned our industrial urban society into a relatively wealthy one —with an extensive and well-off middle class. One effect has been that money has become the relatively available instrument for implementing psychic mobility. Sociologists and historians have long been aware of the role of money as a generalizer of motivation and as an acid solvent of the reciprocal traditional ties that bound men both to their social equals and their "natural superiors." But it must also be recognized that money, especially in the hands of the young, is the agent for rendering real the psychic mobility which the communication revolution generates. It may not be literally true that one can do "anything" in America if one has the money, but one can do a lot.

Generational conflict, though often of necessity covert, is a constant in human history. It is visible in the opening pages of Plato's *Republic,* in Turgenev's *Fathers and Sons,* in Joyce's *Portrait,* in Marquand's *H. M. Pulham, Esq.* But in the past such conflict usually took place under social conditions in which hierachy, scarcity, and less intense communication were characteristic and was therefore more easily contained and eventually guided into an acceptance of the existing order. Today the very education of the young takes place in a context in which the freedom and spontaneity of the youth is relatively emancipated from the structural and ideational conditions inhibiting it in the past. In traditional societies young people advanced from childhood to adulthood along a well-structured road—a series of roles defined and sanctioned by precedent and each role a part of a complex in which it was subordinated to superior roles. Today education takes place under conditions in which the rights and tastes of the young must be taken seriously. The changes we have sketched have, moreover, shaken the certainty of the fathers as well as metamorphosed the docility of the sons, and the result is a critical equality which challenges the current institutions and methods of cultural transmission.

Equality instead of hierarchy; criticism instead of docility; functionally specific instead of generalized sacral authority; free instead of supervised leisure time; psychic mobility instead of traditional rootedness—these come more and more to characterize the condition of our educated and semi-educated youth in America. The standards of the peers now compete with those of the elders; the present competes with the past; spontaneity competes with establishment. Against the domination of age and tradition, youth places its spontaneity and vitality, its own search for the contemporarily meaningful, and even its mass media-whetted taste for novelty.

Such are the developments which have brought about the present condition—the psychological emancipation of large numbers of young people from the past, the older generation, the established institutions, the traditions of family, ethnic group, and church. Moreover, youth, too, is affected by our profound religious crisis. Consequently one can no longer ultimately appeal to religion in the old sense. Religion today often interests the searching youth, but as possible call, not as commanding authority, and indeed as one possible call among many. In this condition the young are not only emancipated, they are also confused. For many of them the problem of meaning whose solution is necessary for the achievement of the "courage to be," the problem of ultimate meaning and its implication for human goals, arises as a poignant existential experience.

HOW THE ADULT SOCIETY APPEARS

The change in America over the last three quarters of a century has been enormous. Perhaps we can characterize that change succinctly by a brief exercise in "sociological etymology." For Aristotle, the word "economics" designated a "science" of household management—the rational basis for allocating scarce elements in the functioning of an *Oikos*. It involved the art of making rational decisions by the householder and was thereby conceived to enhance his freedom and self-determination. For us the word has a vastly changed meaning. It is the study of the laws—impersonal and removed from the control of one man's decisions in the classical case—governing an "economy," that is, a vast structured complex of which we are all a part. No matter that this objective "machine," this "market mechanism," rests ultimately upon individual decisions giving a kind of anonymous and often situationally determined "consumer sovereignty." The vast objective entity dwarfs each individual and appears foreign to him.

Moreover, modern technology has necessitated large-scale work organization so that the process of production itself has become a giant objective structure closely integrated with the market mechanism. The organization of work and distribution have become part of one whole, and the work role has been located within this vast engulfing entity. Technological and economic rationality remain often in conflict, but objectified in the structure of work and distribution, they both remain alienated from the subjective dispositions of human individuals.

Human beings perform in roles—consensually established positions and complexes of behavior which are the basic units of social structures. Roles provide the stage upon which individuals act out the drama of their lives. In all societies roles involve three elements which influence their development. First of all, roles derive a significant part of their structuration from the technical task whose performance they involve. The role of engineer, of teacher, doctor, farmer, plainly show this influence, but it can also be seen in such roles as father, wife, and oldest child. Secondly, roles are part of a complex of other roles —they define human interaction—in work organizations, families, churches, professions with professional-client relationships, etc. As such, the requirements of human organization influence the kinds of demands made upon incumbents. Thirdly, the role must canalize the motivation of individuals behind its ends and its required behavior. To accomplish this it must provide some outlet for human needs and propensities, some expressive opportunities for the individual to act out his own drama. Societies, and roles within a society, obviously differ considerably in the extent to which they place emphasis upon each of these component elements.

The great objective economic and work organizations of our society place the overwhelming emphasis upon the first two of these elements—the technical and the organizational. Roles—careers—designed to meet the needs of economic and technological organization are presented to men as the structured context for their own development. The "career" structured in the organization becomes the mold into which the "biography" must be poured. Not the Confucian "virtuous man," nor the *Imitatio Christi,* nor the Enlightenment of Buddhism, nor the Homeric Achilles, nor the Platonic philosopher-king, nor the 18th century gentleman are to be taken as models for the elicitation and development of human potential. Rather, the succession of roles comprising the promotional system of firm, university, or political career highly influenced by situational and organizational demands provides the effective model. And indeed all the diverse kinds of occupational structures tend to become assimilated to the basic core type, which we now designate as "bureaucracy."

We had earlier cited Max Weber, who protested that though the Puritan wanted to work in a "calling," the men of his own generation were being forced to do so in a secularized calling which had by his day become "an iron cage." Some sociologists profess to see in the secularized "calling" of the present bureaucratic apparatus the continuation not only in form but in spirit as well of the calling of the Protestant Ethic and even the retention of its religious significance. Such a view—obviously ideological in Mannheim's strictest sense—is hard to defend on intellectual grounds. It is a world away from the view of the younger generation. What youth notices bit by bit is that the giant objectification of technical and economic rationality—often in actual conflict and hardly reconciled —begins to look objectively irrational in some essential respects. Its efficiency when measured against anything comparable in the world is still remarkable. For example, in France there are now 310,000 individuals awaiting the installation of telephone service and the average waiting

time is 14 months; in Moscow there are not enough telephone directories to go around; and in Tokyo, installation
costs the equivalent of $450. In the United States, one can
have a phone installed on a few days' notice and for a
modest fee.

Yet the recent publicity over the issue of safety in the
construction of automobiles and the behavior of the com-
panies raise some problems of substantive rationality, let
alone morality. We have all become aware, at least since
President Eisenhower told us to "buy anything," that we
now often consume in order to keep people employed,
thus reversing the ancient formula defining the relationship between working and eating. We all know that the
economy must support a large advertising establishment
to stimulate needs and sustain production, and that this
agency is taste-creating and therefore value-creating, but
that it remains outside the normal demands and controls
made generally upon the agencies of society which create
tastes and values—churches and schools. But most of all
we are aware of the enormous technological potential
which science has placed at our command—that we can
change drastically the conditions of men's lives.

The question of goals and means arises immediately.
How can we make effective use of the present productive
and transformative powers of our technology in a rationally humane manner? One important aspect of that question involves a deeper understanding of the issue that has
dominated so much of our history, the issue of freedom.
It becomes the problem of how we can make life—including work—more conducive to the expression and
realization of the human potential. Must roles—and consequently careers—be modelled so overwhelmingly by the
demands of technology and the demands of organization

maintenance? How can human needs and propensities free themselves from the dominance of what has already been established in our development and seek and develop new forms more rational, more effective, and more humane? If such a question appears "utopian" it is because its distance from strict "rationality" is one of anticipation. It poses problems whose solutions we do not seek, but whose challenge really confronts us. On the other hand, the irrationalities of much of our present situation—our rat race, our embracing of continuous economic growth as a virtue because a necessity under the present organizational forms regardless of the qualitative content of what is produced, our demands for impersonal and inhuman goals of technology and organization—these depart from rationality for other reasons. It is not a matter of anticipation of future challenges and capacities but of a loss of human control over the socio-technical machine we have created.

Reason raises the question of humanizing man's relation to man and man's relation to nature, of humanizing man's living space—the city, for example—and man's design for life. Technological capacity renders such questions anything but utopian, although we see no answers at this stage. Youth, unprecedentedly freed of older restraints in the sphere of social structure and ideas, incomparably more mobile psychically in terms of available models and suggestions for the design of life, critical and reluctant to get into the prepared context, see that that context is more and more irrational. Youth begin to feel that they face an adult occupational system which demands the subordination of their own native aspirations and desires to its functional requirements, but that that system itself does not possess rational or ethical justification in anything like an ultimate sense. Such youth tend more and more to experience the structure of the adult occupational world as alienated from their own interior potentialities, as irrelevant to their inchoate aspirations, and as failing to make sense. It looks to them as though it is largely "phony," lacking in genuineness.

Freer to be themselves, less hemmed in by the formative and regulative consequences of an earlier hierarchical society, they face an objective occupational system which appears to be losing both its self-evidentness and its moral justification. These youth show greater spontaneity and less restraint than earlier generations, greater psychic mobility, and fewer stable moorings. They display a profound reluctance to get into the "iron cage" of the occupational system; they sense the latent possibilities for a more humane life and the decreasing justification of things as they are. Their tendency is toward secession—although perhaps only an episodic secession—from the "establishment," as they call it, and protest against its irrationality, which they often decry as immorality.

What does it mean to say "freer to be themselves"? What is it that comes forward when older restraints are removed? What is the "counter-projection" of a generation which cannot project its motivations into the established occupational structure? To ask the question is to reveal how little we know of the fundamental character of what it means to be human. One thing it apparently is not. It is not John Locke's *tabula rasa,* despite the fact that an entire educational system has been based upon that rather shallow assumption.

But whatever unrecognized human potentials come forward in this situation, they do not and they will not come forward unaffected by the conditions—technological, social, and cultural—of our age. Yet our social science, while contributing considerably to our clarity in analyzing the situation, does not help us much in pointing to causal factors likely to be operative in affecting and influencing the expression of the younger generation in this situation. Sociological theory sees change originating and developing in a many-sided or multifactored situation—social structure, as we have shown above, plays an important part. But so also do situational exigencies (as for example new inventions, population growth, armed aggression, etc., personality characteristics of decision makers and innovators, and the implications of the meanings and values of a culture. For example, a problem of survival may lead to a change in work technique, the precise change may be affected by psychological characteristics of the innovators, and the understanding of the change and how people in general respond to it may be highly influenced by commonly held values. Have there been situational exigencies and have there been innovations whose consequences may influence the attitudes which develop among youth in this new freed condition in which they find themselves?

Marx maintained that productive technology and the consequent relationships of production formed the mentalities of men and affected their predispositions in thought and feeling. That technology has played an important part in making the occupational system what it is seems clear enough. It has been suggested recently that we should look more closely at the technology of communications. We have suggested above that the communications revolution brings about a vast increase in psychic mobility. Marshall McLuhan would suggest that such a view, while not necessarily incorrect, is gross and depends too exclusively on the effect of content. McLuhan states that the various media of communication have different and quite specific effects upon the mentality of their users. For him communication technology is qualitatively decisive.

McLuhan suggests that the new generation has been formed by the new media, that they have a different kind of mentality, a different propensity to relate to the world, a different way of perceiving and responding to the world that is the product of electronic or electric communication media. He suggests a replacement of the Comtian triad—religious phase, metaphysical phase, positive phase—by another. He sees traditional societies as those in which the oral medium of communication is predominant and nearly exclusive. They are pre-alphabetical in any effective sense. The result is a personality type—so he maintains—in which experience is mediated through an internal balance of the senses different from that prevailing in a literate society. Long years of the alphabet—especially intensified by print—have led to a visual dominance in the internal sense-ratio with its Euclidian space, its perspective, its peculiar quantification of life, its functional and consequent emotional fragmentation. All of this is greatly intensified by print, with its structural essentials of repeatability, continuity, and lineality. This dominance of a particular sense—visual in modern Western society, audio-tactile in traditional societies—is related to and determined by the changing technology of communication. Writing, and especially printing, isolated sight and made it dominant, and thereby disrupted the old oral and audio-tactile cultures.

However, it is McLuhan's hypothesis—he rather proclaims it as a fact—that electronic media are leading to a new rearrangement of the individual sense hierarchies in our society. Especially important is television, with its incomplete image. Electronic media are bringing back audio-tactile dominance and all the propensities of thinking, feeling, and acting that go with it. For Comte's "religious—metaphysical—positive" stages, McLuhan proposes "audio-tactile" (like Comte's religious), and related to the oral medium, visual consisting of both a manuscript and a printing stage (the former corresponding to Comte's second, the latter to his third state), and now a reversal unforeseen by Comte and brought about by electronic media—a new audio-tactile period. We live at present in the confusing transition. McLuhan says that the contemporary hiatus in education is the consequence of the fact that teachers are print products and students have been formed by the new electronic media. Teachers are, to use the colorful oral language of some of McLuhan's disciples, "pobs." (Print-oriented bastards.)

This is a complex and a sophisticated hypothesis and one as yet little analyzed and clarified, let alone tested. But it obviously says something of significance to the effort to understand social change in our day. For our subject, it implies that within the situation whose basic structure we have delineated, new factors are at work which bring about subtle subliminal changes of the greatest significance. If indeed this hypothesis contains important germs of historic truth—if the development from *mythos* to *logos*, from traditional society to modernity is being reversed in significant respects—then the present generational conflict so freely expressed in the new situation of egalitarian levelling contains elements fraught with significance for the future remaking of society and culture.

If new modes of experiencing and responding to the world are developing, the task of social science is to comprehend them and to render them available to our understanding. We need to understand how these effects are wrought, and their behavioral significance. The profound reluctance of our literate youth to enter the iron cage may in fact be aggravated by a changed mode of experience. Could it be that the youth from our deprived and underprivileged minorities who give so heroic an account of themselves in Vietnam are basically "pre-alphabetical," or at least "pre-print," in their mentalities and response patterns, having come from cultural enclaves where the audio-tactile still predominates? Can it be that the school did not effect a great interiorization of print-culture, and that electronic media built upon what the family and early culture had already deposited in their psyches? Can it be also that our literate youth have partially internalized the print-culture in their schools and their middle class home milieu, but that their affluent exposure to the new media under the conditions of decreasing hierarchical influence makes them "nonpobs" as well? The former can achieve significance in war while the latter hesitate in their freedom, caught between two worlds. These are all questions; we do not have the answers to them, any more than to the questions raised in the next chapter.

V

Christianity and the Atheism
of Contemporary Youth

Every questionnaire administered on the subject in America reports an overwhelming majority of people declaring that they believe in God. When they are subsequently asked other questions which would inquire into what they believe to be the practical implications of their declared theistic faith, they often reveal that their belief in God has little significance in practice for them. Both in America and elsewhere, there are other people who, although they disclaim belief in God, find life meaningful and seek to live it responsibily. For example, sincere Marxists appear to find in their notion of "history" a human project that both gives direction to their lives and possesses ethical implication for their behavior.[1] There are also those of whom Harvey Cox speaks who experience no fall from innocence in contemporary unbelief because they have never believed; who do not understand what Tillich means by the problem of meaninglessness because it never occurred to them that things had any ultimate meaning or any meaning not simply attributed to them by men.[2] There are, of course, sincere Christians, and adherents of other faiths as well, who believe seriously and act upon the implications of their convictions.

How many young people today fit into these categories we have no way of knowing. Probably a majority fit into some version of them. But a newer point of view among youth has also become apparent. This newer outlook is diagnostically of considerable significance. It throws light, once understood, on some of the deeper problems of religion in our day.

It is not possible in this situation to arrive at a meaningful definition of atheism and to state adequately what conversion from atheism to Christianity would involve. Therefore, we shall have to devise a more indirect way of getting at the issues. First, we shall present a summary of the important ideas about religion of several intellectual figures of the recent past. We select these particular figures not because we necessarily attribute a casual significance to their ideas but because we believe them representative of ideas and attitudes widely associated with unbelief among young people today. Second, we shall sample some studies and observations concerning the situation of youth in America. Then we shall try to look briefly at the historical background of both the ideas we have presented and the current situation we have roughly sketched. This procedure should suggest to us at least some general idea of where young people in America are; where they stand in terms of sociological and historical dimensions of their situation. It is hoped that such a strategy will reveal to us what many young people feel and believe; that it will enable us to catch some glimpse of how they see their world.

One hears complaints from college administrators, members of the faculty, and from churchmen that they cannot comprehend people "under thirty." It is the conviction of the present author that such complaints amount to the admission that these people do not understand our recent history and consequently fail to see what is happening in America today. It is a basic premise of this chapter that the behavior of "way-out" youth is quite comprehensible because it is a response to an existing situation. Moreover, if their elders really knew all along and believed all along what they quite obviously claimed to know and believe, then they should have expected this reaction.

Since we cannot define atheism with any precision, let us attempt to describe, from a sociological perspective, a central core characteristic of religion. I say from a sociological perspective because I shall try to offer a characteristic of religion that is most important functionally both to the individual and to his society. You will recall that Schleiermacher saw the central core element in religion to be the experience of absolute dependence. This definition has often been criticized as over-simplified and insufficient. Despite the truth of these criticisms, however, Schleiermacher makes a significant point. Religion does involve a kind of relationship; it involves a relationship to a realm that transcends the sphere of the ordinary.

But here I would call attention to another side of the matter. Man does not simply enter into a religious relation but his religion becomes significant for his action in the world. Seen from this point of view, a strategic core element of religion is that it contributes a sense of ontologically justified orientation. The word "sense" implies both feeling and cognition. The word "ontological" means that the orientation not only points out how man may locate and direct his life but that such orientation is built into the structure of things. It is not a mere projection, convention, or illusion. The convinced Christian and the convinced Marxist both possess this. What distinguishes religion from such religious surrogates as communism and nationalism are other things;[3] they both possess this core element.

Such a sense of ontologically justified orientation for life, may be simply parrotting of widely held conventions, that is, it may, in Heidegger's terms, be "inauthentic." Or it may be a deep conviction genuinely held by the individual; it may be "authentic."[4] Moreover, it may be spontaneous and unquestioned; the possession of the "once born," to use William James's term. Or it may be wrested from tragedy and despair by a leap of faith and be maintained by resolve.

Let us now examine briefly some of the representative figures of contemporary unbelief against the background of this core element. First, there was Ludwig Feuerbach, whom Marx and Engels hailed as a liberator (cf. Chapter Two).[5] According to Feuerbach, belief in God was the projection of man's interior nature into the void outside. In this process man conceives of his own essence as an object outside and above himself and thereby turns himself into the creature of that object. In this consists man's alienation from himself. In this is man damaged and robbed of the capacity to take responsibility for his own self-development and self-fulfillment. Religion was the institutional form in which this alienating theism subsisted in human society. The emancipation of man required its destruction. Theism was denied in the name of emancipation and self-realization. This suggests that for some, at least, religion was experienced as a form of thralldom and inhibition.

Nietzsche is perhaps the most extreme of the 19th century rejectors of Christianity. To Nietzsche, an equivocal attitude toward Christianity was itself an offense. Christianity must be refused outright; it must be responded to with "the absolute no." Christianity is also seen by Nietzsche as an unconscious process of projection. Man is afraid of accepting as his own his latent possibilities of power and love and so he projects them outside as the characteristics of an imaginary being. In so doing, man splits himself in two—a weak part which he recognizes as man, as himself; a strong part which he calls God. Thus man frustrates his own possibilities. The destruction of Christianity, thought Nietzsche, was a supreme task for the men of his time. Human liberation meant becoming God's assassins. Then man could realize the secret possibilities that slumbered within him.[6]

Sigmund Freud also saw religion as a matter of human projection, but of a projection that was not only unconscious but infantile. Freud felt that men experienced in life the vast uncertainty of human existence—man's helplessness in an indifferent or even hostile world. This human condition elicited from men the unconscious acting out of infantile motivations; triggered off the re-enactment of an archaic drama recalled from infancy. Man's helplessness had, in Freud's words, "an infantile prototype." Says Freud, "Once before one has been in such a state of helplessness: as a little child in relationship to one's parents. For one had reason to fear them, especially the father, though at the same time one was sure of his protection against the dangers then known to one." In this situation, "man makes the forces of nature not simply in the image of men with whom he can associate as equals —that would not do justice to the overpowering impression they make on him—but he gives them characteristics of the father, makes them into gods," thereby following "an infantile prototype."

Freud felt that man was a lost being in a hostile world, and although he emphasized the functional role of religion in making men work instead of seeking pleasure and keeping public order in the face of human passions, he nevertheless felt that religion "had to go" and that men should put away childish things. For he felt, in his manifest reasoning at least, that our helplessness was hardly helped by religion and that our behavior despite religion left much to be desired. Man should therefore give up this infantile projection, recognizing its illusory character. When he does this, he will not find himself happy or with his problems solved, rather he "will find himself in a difficult situation," having to admit that he is ultimately utterly helpless and not the center of creation. But, asks Freud, "Is it not the destiny of childishness to be overcome?"[7]

For Jean-Paul Sartre also, God is but a projection of man's unfulfilled and indeed impossible ambitions and aspirations. Man, according to Sartre, tries in history to do away with his radical contingency and his basic non-relatedness to the world. Sartre sees man as a "futile passion"; sees him consisting basically in an absence of structure, an openness, as "freedom." Man's existence precedes his essence. He is basically open to the possibility of being thrown into the world and there abandoned to his own intelligence and efforts. For Sartre this openness, this liberty, is pointless. Man's project is absurd and meaningless. Yet man must create his own essence; each man must do it for himself. Sartre feels that alone, and with no basic communication with others, each man must take the responsibility to make himself. He must become engaged. But in all this God has no place.[8]

Finally, we shall consider Albert Camus. Camus saw the world without God as absurd. After a long spiritual odyssey that is supposed to have brought him at one point close to conversion to Catholicism, he found no traces of God either in the creation or in human history. Man he saw locked in absurd immanence with no window on transcendence as its redeeming feature. Yet Camus was chiefly a moralist. He raised moral questions for man and history. Man, he felt, must take his situation seriously. He must act responsibly to make human existence humane. He must take moral responsibility.[9]

The basic attitude toward the traditional belief in God to be seen in these thinkers is quite similar to that found among many young people today. Christianity, in its traditional forms, seems entirely foreign to them. To some, closer to it, it is incredible. To others, removed by a generation or more from belief, it is incomprehensible. But this alienation from religion and its world view and attitudes toward sacred things is not the whole picture. These young people are also often skeptical with respect to mundane things—with respect to quite prosaic bourgeois mundane things. The job, the goals of society, marriage, and the family—all are subject to some suspicion, the object of questioning and doubt as we have pointed out earlier.

One of the most subtle and significant of the supports of a society is being called into question in our day. Societies have always rested at base upon the obvious and unquestioned rightness of things as they are. An unquestioned consensus upon the validity of institutions and norms, the self-evidentness of the order of social things, permeated society. Even rebels did not question at the most fundamental level. The Marxist revolutionary saw capitalism doing badly what should be done, but he agreed to a startling extent with the capitalist about what obviously should be done.

But now some young people—how many we do not know—question the very fundamental values upon which American society has long rested. The basic psychological substrate of society has come into consciousness, and once conscious, it has come to appear far less self-evident than it did to those who saw it as part of the inevitable ontological landscape. The basic matter of value consensus is becoming problematic for many of our youth. For those young people who still believe or who are still under the influence of religion, these ideas of the others are quite real as well. They feel the need to judge their own religious attitudes to some degree by the demands of such ideas. To understand this situation among young people today let us look briefly at some current observations.

Kenneth Kenniston did a study of young people who were severely alienated, who distrusted and rejected their American culture, and who saw in non-commitment a way of life. These were well-to-do youth at an elite college, but they came out of home backgrounds which predisposed them to reject many current American values. They exhibited a strong dislike of competition and a marked reluctance with respect to the adult male role.

Kenniston says,

The family experiences of these youths instilled in them a deep and usually unconscious conviction of the undesirability of adult maleness, and therefore of adulthood in general. At the most personal and unconscious level, this conviction stems partly from the image of their own fathers as weak, easily defeated and controlled, damaged by and unable to defend themselves against women. And another part of this conviction stems from the subjects' own childhood experiences with "masculine assertiveness" and the unintended consequences of their competition with their fathers: aggressiveness, competitiveness, initiative, and rivalry—all qualities usually considered desirable among men in our society—had here led to disastrous results. Furthermore, the struggle for a woman's exclusive love resulted merely in being limited and bound by her. This "lesson" persists into early adulthood, when the alienated still find themselves afraid of reciprocated intimacy with a woman. All of these largely unconscious themes of childhood—the view of men as weak, damaged and controlled, the fears of aggression and competition, the image of women as controlling and destructive to men—cooperated to produce a highly negative view of adulthood.[10]

These young people saw their fathers, who were often quite successful in the public world, as failures in life and decided not to let themselves be victimized by the world as their fathers were.

Erikson had earlier pointed out how societies make use of the residues of childhood to organize and canalize the motivation of adults in the context of adult roles. Kenniston finds these residues of childhood experiences molded and shaped into adult expression by "the social circumstances" of the lives of these students. Important among these he names, "being talented and relatively privileged Americans attending an elite college, being members of a highly technological society, living in a world changing at an enormously rapid rate, participating in a long tradition of intellectual skepticism, being products of a special kind of family system. These circumstances help determine what becomes of the legacy of childhood . . ."[11] He finds these youth giving themselves up to a cult of the present. "Whatever conscious meaning their lives may have is given by immediacy, experience, the here and now."[12]

This cult of the present finds passive expression in the "search for sentience." It finds active expression in the "search for a breakthrough." "The alienated value must be those moments when the barriers to perception crumble, when the walls between themselves and the world fall away and they are 'in contact' with nature, other people, or themselves."[13] Of course, such break-throughs are relatively rare. The search for such a break-through involves the "conviction of alienated subjects that they are *constricted by conventional categories,* impris-oned by the usual ways of seeing the world, of coping with their own feelings and fantasies, of dealing with other people, even of channeling inner impulse into activity."[14]

The meaning of the cult of the present for these young men is complex. In part, it is a response to a conscious desire to escape their pasts and avoid their futures, but it is more than this. The alienated feel hemmed in and constrained by their worlds (and, unconsciously, by their unruly fantasies and feelings); they reject the culture which shaped them; they chafe under even the ordinary categories through which most men filter experience and feeling. To some extent, they are incapable of employing these categories, for their experience has disposed them to see the world differently; but in part, their ideology dictates that they should *choose* to reject these categories. They are extraordinarily aware of the blinders of selective awareness and inattention which many men use to hide the seamier sides of their lives from themselves; and though the alienated have, in fact, blinders of their own, they are at least different and unconventional blinders.[15]

Kenniston continues,

The cult of the present is, however, not only a theme of alienation but is found in other forms among many young people. Indeed, among the defining characteristics of American youth culture—the special world of American adolescents and young adults—are a concentration on the present, a focus on immediate experience, an effort to achieve "genuineness," "directness," "sincerity," in perception and human relations. We see this cult in both forms—as a search for external stimulation and for internal transformation—in many of the deviant behaviors of our society: in the search for adventure among delinquent gangs, in the use of drugs to break through the gates of perception, in the "beat" quest for "kicks." And in less extreme forms, a similar emphasis on the present exists in the increasing American stress on consumption rather than saving, on the "rich, full life" in the present rather than the deferred goals and future satisfactions of an earlier society. All of this suggests that the alienated are reacting to a problem which transcends the particularities of their individual lives, and that the cult of the present is a response to historical pressures which affect alienated and unalienated alike.[16]

Moreover, without any commitment to the things around them, the alienated develop only a partial and fragmented identity. They tend to see commitments as claims made upon them, and they see claims as destructive. Moreover, they tend to experience their freedom as a burden. Here it must be stressed that I am characterizing the findings of Kenniston's study, not the ideas of Jean-

Paul Sartre! Kenniston says further, "At root, probably the most powerful unconscious motive in many of these young men is their desire to merge, to fuse with, to lose themselves in some embracing person, experience, or group. This *fantasy of mystical union* involves an unconscious desire to lose all selfhood in some undifferentiated state with another or with nature, to be totally embraced and to embrace totally."[17] This desire to merge underlies their fear of commitment and increases it, since they fear this desire to lose identity lurking within them.

Kenniston also sees some evidence that the alienated engage in a quest for positive values.[18] They suspect the way things are in a basic way. They tend to judge any belief by the motives they see beneath it. They consciously suffer from what "they sense as the *impossibility of certainty*," underneath which there "lies a less conscious and contrasting feeling, a *yearning for absolutes*."

Here, too, Kenniston sees the alienated not totally different from large numbers of the general run but exaggerating their characteristics. He states:

We are dealing not only with a problem in individual psychology but with the impact on individual lives of problems created by our social and intellectual history. The outlooks of the alienated are clearly related to the intellectual currents of our time and are but a slight exaggeration of intellectual trends in which we all take part. An inability to find viable and enduring positive values is common to many, and perhaps most, Americans; distrust of ideology and utopian thinking is found among most of the leading thinkers of our day; the tendency to emphasize the arbitrary subjectivity of values and their role in masking self-interest, class position, libidinal drive, or existential anxiety is shared by most of the prevalent philosophies of the twentieth century. The alienated problem of finding positive values both reflects and points to comparable problems in our culture as a whole.[19]

Nathan Leites once pointed out that many philosophical positions resembled psychological disorders in that they represented a certain perspective upon and attitude toward the world. We see this resemblance again in Kenniston's study. These attitudes are not simply caused by the childhood residues. The childhood residues predispose the individual to one direction of development rather than another. But the current pressures of the adult society play an important part in directing development too. Kenniston emphasizes this contemporary character of the alienated response while showing the predisposing role of the childhood residues. He shows that "chronic change" is an important element; he points also to the tendency for work to lose its meaning.

Speaking no longer of the alienated subjects of his study but of the normal college youth from among whom his subjects were drawn, he states that although these more ordinary youth generally approve of American society, or at least accept it as "simply there," they are nevertheless quite unenthusiastic participants in it.

But at the same time, these young men and women often show a lack of deep commitment to adult values and roles. They are not alienated as are beatniks, delinquents, or our group of alienated students. Rather, they view the adult world they expect to enter with a subtle distrust, a lack of high expectations, hopes, or dreams, and an often unstated feeling that they will have to "settle" for less than they would hope for if they let themselves hope. A surprising number, despite their efforts to get good grades so that they can get into good graduate schools and eventually have good careers, despite their manifest desire to do well in the existing social order, nonetheless view it, in Paul Goodman's phrase, as "an apparently closed room with a rat race going on in the middle." Whether they call it a rat race or not is immaterial (though many half-jokingly do); the point is that they expect little in the way of personal fulfillment, growth, or creativity from their future roles in the public world. Essentially, they recognize that adulthood is a relatively cold, demanding, specialized and abstracted world where "meaningful" work is so scarce they do not even ask for it. Thus the majority stay "cool" when it comes to the "real world"; and "coolness" means above all detachment, lack of emotion, absence of deep commitment, not being either enthusiastic or rejecting adulthood.[20]

Another study done by two sociologists at the University of California at Santa Barbara suggests a similar mental landscape for the "hippies." They speak of "an emerging new ethos" which is "cool and irreverent" and "reflects a good deal of disaffection toward many of our more traditional roots." Simmons and Winograd state, "The emerging ethic is hang-loose in a number of senses, but, its deep-running feature is that things once taken for granted as God-given or American constitution-given— those basic premises about the world and the way it works —are no longer taken for granted or given automatic allegiance. In other words, many Americans are hanging a bit loose from traditional Americana."[21] Yet the authors find "ill-formed and vaguely expressed" basic values in this outlook. They find irreverence, humanism, spontaneity, tolerance, rejection of the establishment, and sympathy for the underdog important among them. As a matter of fact, it is only perhaps in the sexual sphere, where a much less inhibited but nevertheless personal kind of behavior is approved, that it differs fundamentally from the basic Christian values. It deviates from the way those values are found in its anti-establishment and hang-loose character. The raw material of the older order is reworked. But it *is* an ethos and an ethic of secession from the *status quo*. In that, too, it may be said to resemble the original Christian interim ethic. But it obviously and strikingly lacks the hope that earlier ethos and ethics exhibited so impressively.

Let us look briefly at one more evaluation of the present position of youth. Paul Goodman, viewing the way our society has developed as an autonomous structure based upon premises which often bear only the most remote resemblance to their institutional consequences, has stated that youth born after the second world war often experience the world of the adults as absurd. But, perhaps, most significant is his suggestion that among that which is missing for youth is the chance to grow up in a manly job and with a basic faith.

Says Goodman, "The sense that life is going on, and the confidence that the world will continue to support the next step of it, is called faith. It is hard to grow up without faith. For then one is subject to these nagging unanswerable questions: Am I worthless? How can I prove myself? What chance is there for me? Did I ever have a chance?" Goodman feels that real faith and real vocation are being lost, that it is part of the "weakening of the sense that there is a nature of things." And he characterizes what is happening among youth as the creation of two great groups,

the bright young men wasted in the rat race and the bright young men increasingly unused and thwarted as independents . . . Desperately, then, people may try to fill the void of worthlessness-and-abandonment by seeking money or status, or by busy work, or by self-proving exploits, both to silence critics and to silence one's own doubts. They substitute role playing, conforming, and belonging for the grace of meeting objective opportunity. But there is no justification in such "works," for they are not really the man's own works, nor God's providence for him . . . Or alternately, people may spurn the false roles that are available and try for formless mystical experiences . . . Or alternately, again, where the despair of abandonment is acute, as with many juveniles, they rush fatalistically to punishment, to have it over with and be received back.[22]

This returns us to our earlier observation. The evidence suggests a vast and affluent American society based upon a fantastically successful scientific technology. It points to a society with a highly elaborated and highly standardized, highly objectified, occupational system whose roles prove to be tremendously demanding upon those in its middle and upper reaches. Moreover, this demandingness is not simply a matter of technological difficulty but primarily derived from organizational and sociological dilemmas built into the structure by its past history. The evidence suggests that this impressive sociological apparatus is losing its rootedness in the outlooks and motivational structure of the new generation! The job no longer beckons as the exciting and stimulating challenge; it no longer can demand total devotion; no longer elicit fervent activity and repay with high self-esteem. Competition no longer seems so significant a trial, and success no longer so attractive a reward. What is really happening? Let us look back for a few moments at our immediate history.

This situation did not fall from the sky. It is the result

of the developments of the past decades, of the past two centuries. Let us begin by asking where Christianity was in the background situation out of which this condition seems to have developed. The fact is that since the French Revolution, if not longer, Christianity was, on the continent, being pushed farther and farther from the vital centers of Western life. The great attempt of Protestantism in Germany in the 19th century to confront modernity and maintain its own relevance was far from successful.

In England, the same thing was taking place in the last years of the 18th and the first of the 19th century as was taking place in France, but in a less dramatic and more gradual English way. On Easter Sunday of 1803, there were three persons present in St. Paul's Cathedral in London. Methodism arose as a protest against the dessication of religion in the 18th century and the near demise of the English church caused by the subtle suffusion of deism, and as the desire to rekindle the fires of an engaged and devout Christianity.

In America, a native gregariousness, characteristic of our history, and the consequence of revivalism kept the church alive, but as early as the year 1800 popular rationalist works, like Thomas Paine's *Age of Reason,* had penetrated far into the American rural hinterland.

Earlier chapters have pointed out how much the Christian churches—Roman Catholic, Lutheran, and Anglican —were deeply and securely bound up with the old order which was violently replaced by the revolution and which was rendered obsolete forever by the Industrial Revolution. These two great transformations—the second a continuing process now taking place throughout the world; the first a violent and volatile surfacing of deep historic impulses toward democracy and equality, also still continuing in our day—destroyed the context in which Christianity had become part of the everyday society and the ordinary lives of men.

The churches were, by and large, overidentified with and almost inextricably involved in the old order both in the ordinary life of the people and in the realm of culture and thought. They tended to see the inevitable attempts to break out of this older situation, which had become intolerable to strategic classes in the European community, as destructive and to be always "too little and too late" in their attempts to adapt to them.

Calvinism did better. It enabled a new middle class to develop and Christianize an evolving identity. But this too led to secularization and the abandonment of the older beliefs or else it hardened—as in the more fundamentalist Calvinist groups—into an intransigent verbal literalism, reactive and defensive in its response to evolving modernity. Whether or not this predicament of the churches could have been prevented, given the cultural situation and the means of understanding and adjustment available to men at the time, seems doubtful. That they have not responded to its aftermath with much imagination and creativity is surely not to be doubted.

The Age of Enlightenment was not a glorious period in the history of any of the churches. Its depreciation of religious enthusiasm ["Enthusiasm" in the eighteenth century to many good Anglican deists meant Methodism!] is notorious, and it cannot be pretended that the absence of fanaticism was accorded the recompense of solid and profound virtue. It was a time when "it was easy to talk of the loftiest virtues without practicing even the lowliest." It was an age of rationalism in the sense that the capacity of the self-enlightened human intellect to settle all the problems that were presented to it was hardly doubted. The temper of philosophy was cold and static; the vast enrichment of the field of empirical knowledge, which was to come to fruition in the next century, was almost unsuspected. Its intellectual constructions were at once artificial and superficial. In literature, classicism reigned supreme; all novelty and freshness were severely discountenanced. The churches retained their established positions, and they were content to live on their past. The practice of religion, such as it was, was conventional. The traditional theology, whether in its Catholic or Protestant form, was moribund, and the writers and thinkers of the time, even if for the sake of propriety they treated it with a patronizing tolerance, in effect ignored its claim on their allegiance.[23]

It was this world whose shaky structure was brought tumbling down by the French Revolution. It was this world which the Industrial Revolution, and the mass industrial society it initiated, destroyed irrevocably among the Western people. What happened in the social and political life of peoples happened also in their intellectual life. C. C. J. Webb has said, "Kant had done in the sphere of thought what the French Revolution had done in politics. He had brought down the long tottering edifice of the established order and had made a new start possible by clearing the ground once and for all of an inveterate growth of old pretensions to transcend the common lot of man."[24] To the influence of political ideas and of philosophy must be added that of science. Both in the sphere of a transformed understanding of the world and of man and as the basis for applied technology, science transformed man's inner and outer worlds.

In America, the revival of religion after the American Revolution, which was stimulated by the Second Great Awakening and of the successive revivals which came in its wake, continued into the second half of the 19th century. Yet, secularizing influences asserted themselves more and more, bringing about what Merle Curti characterized as a marked "delimitation of the supernatural" in American thinking.[25] Culture in America was decisively influenced both in form and content by the Enlightenment heritage and by the progress of science and its attendant ideologies. Moreover, the older ascetic attitude toward life weakened. Already in the first half of the 19th century there was to be seen in America what Henry Adams characterized as the growing cheerfulness of religion. Key Calvinist notions were given up even earlier in favor of free will and the convictions of the possibilities of self-determination.[26] As the century drew to a close, secularization and revolt against older standards became increasingly apparent. Socially mobile Americans, moving from farms and rural communities to urban environments and occupations, revolted against the narrowness of the older rural Protestantism or the "Victorianism" of more sedate small town life.

Today, continuing social mobility in the post World War II period, unprecedented affluence, and the venture of mass higher education bring the results of this complex European and American history into the personal lives of great numbers of American youth. They do so in the context of a highly urbanized society, a society characterized by chronic rapid change, a society without deep traditional roots and whose traditional roots, such as they are, are being rapidly destroyed. The old ideas have long been questioned by an elite; now they are being questioned by masses in our educational system. The old ways of life were always rejected by some for a variety of reasons; now they are being rejected by an articulate and visible minority and being questioned by many more. The way things are appears neither satisfactory nor self-evidently justified. The critical ideas of our heritage stand available for use as weapons against a society that no longer fits the emerging predispositions and, as yet, amorphous desires and wishes of its youth.

This is really the world of the secular city. It is not made up of the workaday unthinking secularized ex-Protestants of Harvey Cox's presentation alone. It is made up of their sons and daughters who begin to question its very foundations. These doubts and questionings can no longer be thought of as simply the usual behavior of the youth culture. They present a more serious phenomenon than that. It does assume the styles of passing fads and will continue to do so, but beneath the changing externals of its expression the youth are passing judgment upon their society. There are still many for whom the conventions, based upon past convictions, provide a kind of context and that context provides some guidelines for human orientation and choice. Cox's secular man with no need for meaning is still there; he is Heidegger's *Das Man*. But malaise, reluctance to assume adult roles, loss of orientation, search for meaning and direction, rebellion against the adult society, a cult of experience and of the present—all these testify to the loss of meaning. All these testify that we witness a spiritual crisis. The incapacity of our spiritual and intellectual leaders to offer meaning to these youth is a further testimony. The trumpet gives an uncertain sound, when indeed one can hear it at all.

In America, the vast objective structure of the occupational and status system, and the value system that supports it, are losing their resonance in the souls of American youth. There is a degree of secession taking place and a much larger sympathy for secession. The secession and wish for secession among our educated youth, the products of our mass higher education, which was once seen as the agency for realizing the American dream, is real. Something like this happened once before in Western history.

At the time of the Reformation, important elements of the middle classes found the vast objectified clerical structure, ritual and sacramental system, and rationalized theology of the Old Church increasingly meaningless. Indeed, they experienced it as a barrier to their living experience and their self-realization. They too were a minority; in some cases quite a small minority. But they belong to strategic groups in society—to the intellectuals, the leaders of government, and the commercial and trading classes.

The seceding youth of today may price themselves out of the picture by the impossible demands they make upon the present system. Many of them may have to "settle" for things as they are. But those who settle, together with their sympathizers—basically disaffected and accepting what they feel they cannot avoid—will certainly enter strategic centers of influence and decision in our society. Their secession, too, is sure to have its effect.

This revolt is not just some kind of subjective aberration of young Americans. In fact, a close look at the objective situation will reveal that it is in many fundamental respects quite justified. It is true that the reasons often advanced by those involved are not too convincing; it is also true that the modes of quest for alternatives often seem blind and ineffective. But it is difficult to doubt that there is solid objective justification for this secession. The development of a secular culture has emptied out the ancient meanings for many. The institutions charged with the custody of these ancient meanings have not kept pace with change and have not developed the capacity to present their beliefs as relevant. The older external structure of business, government, and education remain. But youth stands before them reluctant.

Talcott Parsons has characterized American society as one in which the activity involved in "adaptation," that is, in work, organization, and management, is highly valued and given both material and immaterial rewards. The goal has become less significant. The American occupational system came to give work—in itself and not as a reasonable means to desirable ends—an autonomous approval. The occupational role became central to the self-definition and self-regard of the adult male. In it he continually proved himself. In his job, he continually validated himself by achievement. Favoritism, fraud, and frivolity corrupt this picture, but what this picture shows us has long been a central element in our occupational system. The middle class world was largely based upon this occupational commitment.[27] The world of that large and strategic group of Americans was one where a man was defined by what he "did," and where people had not simply biographies but careers. The career was a life plan embedded in the hierarchical structure of the occupational system. With its ranks and way stations, it was the path to success or locus of failure.

It has now become commonplace to admit that Christianity played an important part in preparing for this kind of occupational system. In the Protestant and notably Calvinist notion of the "calling" or "vocation" in the world as the expression of an inner-worldly asceticism, Max Weber and many other sociologists following him see the roots of the secular occupational career system of our time. Work as the organized expression of life's most meaningful activity and the deferment of present satisfaction for future goals, both decisive for this occupational system, derive from such Christian antecedents.

To simplify greatly a complex set of historical developments, what seems to have transpired is something on this order. Those middle class groups that embraced Calvinism came to find meaning in their lives in the context of their work in the world, seen as a "calling." In this calling, they sought to do God's will and at the same time reassure themselves of their spiritual condition. They repressed, so far as possible, all spontaneity and frivolity, avoided all erotic or sensuous pleasures, and tried to mobilize all their human energies behind the demands of their calling. This inner-worldly asceticism, as Weber called it, served two purposes. It provided sober, steadfast, daily work in a calling—the phrase is Weber's—a useful ascetic discipline to subdue the flesh and resist the devil. It also fulfilled man as God's instrument, building, in his humble way and without understanding how, God's Kingdom.

The uncertainty attending the idea of predestination gave rise to the doctrine of evidences. Men sought for signs that they might know where they stood. Proper ascetic behavior was a sign of grace, since a human nature totally depraved could not bring it about. Therefore, if one behaved well, it indicated that one was of the elect. In time, this was materialized into seeing the signs of election in economic success. A form of self-validation, through ascetic discipline directed into work in the world, became central for middle class activity. The deferment of immediate gratification for future rewards was also promoted by the austere Calvinist ethic. Here we have the theological foundation for the righteous behavior of the regenerate middle class. Weber saw this as one—one among many— strategic factor in bringing about the kind of occupational system we have today. While this Weberian hypothesis is obviously over-simplified, it does suggest an important element in the complex development.

Weber points out that, once this structure was erected, it became self-sufficient. With the secularization of society, it no longer possessed its old theological justification, but with the notion of self-validation by achievement built into the system and accepted in itself as a general value— the continuing high cultural evaluation of work—such theological justification was superfluous. Western middle classes had deeply internalized the behavioral implications of the Calvinistic ethic. Sober, steadfast, daily work in a career—a career which was central to a man's selfhood —became habit in William James's sense; it became a second nature.

This is not the whole picture; that such occupational structures developed in the university in Lutheran Germany and in Catholic countries like France suggests a more complex problem than Weber poses. Yet, the suppression of aesthetic, expressive, and erotic sides of culture in the Anglo-Saxon countries and the concentration on the value of work goes farther than in other countries. Pre-industrial humane culture remained important in the continental nations in a way not true of 19th century America or even England.

Matthew Arnold, who saw the sea of faith receding that night on Dover Beach, also saw English culture being choked by the repression of its Hellenic elements by the Hebraic. Weber later on also came to agree with the kind of anti-Puritan stand taken by Arnold. He stated:

The Puritan wanted to work in a calling; we are forced to do so. For when asceticism was carried out of monastic cells into everyday life and began to dominate wordly morality, it did its part in building the tremendous cosmos of the modern economic order. This order is now bound to the technical and economic conditions of machine production which today determines the lives of all the individuals who are born into this mechanism, not only those directly concerned with economic acquisition, with irresistible force. Perhaps it will so determine them untl the last ton of fossilized coal is burnt. In Baxter's view the care for external goods should lie on the shoulders of the "saint" like a light cloak which can be thrown aside at any moment. *But fate decreed that the cloak should become an iron cage.*

Since asceticism undertook to remodel the world and to work out its ideals in the world, material goods have gained an increasing and finally inexorable power over the lives of men as at no previous period in history . . . *No one knows who will live in this cage in the future,* or whether at the end of this tremendous development *entirely new prophets* will arise, or there will be a great *rebirth of old ideas and ideals,* or, if neither, mechanized petrification, embellished with a sort of convulsive importance. For of the last stage of this development, it might truly be said, *"Specialists without spirit, sensualists without heart";* this nullity imagines that it has attained a level civilization never before achieved.[28]

Is the view of our seceding youth so different from that anticipated by Max Weber? Weber saw the system ending with these characteristics, characteristics meriting the epithets, "specialists without spirit, sensualists without heart." Recall Kenniston speaking not of his alienated subjects but the larger group of their fellows at an elite college, "They recognize that adulthood is a relatively cold, demanding, specialized, and abstracted world where 'mean-

ingful' work is so scarce they do not even ask for it."[29]
Says Weber, "Mechanized petrification, embellished with
a sort of convulsive importance." Says Paul Goodman,
"They substitute role playing, conforming, and belonging
for the grace of meeting objective opportunity. But there
is no justification in such 'works,' for they are not really
the man's own works, nor God's providence for him."[30]
Says Weber, "This nullity imagines that it has attained a
level of civilization never before achieved."

Simmons and Winograd reproduce the thinking of the
"hippies" in this way, "Who's going to be left to run the
world if everybody turns on? . . . Who will hold the world
together? Maybe nobody will hold the *present* world
together. Who wants to? How much of it do we really
need? How many of our proud items are only consolation
prizes? Maybe a newer social order could evolve in which
we would have real things that we talk about on rainy
nights but never seem to achieve."[31]

Earlier we defined an essential core element in religion
as a sense of ontologically justified orientation. Obviously
the Calvinistic notion of the calling provided that. Its
automatic continuation, its functional autonomy as part
of the social system and the motivational system of the
middle class, after secularization, also continued to provide it for some time. But the ascetic aspects of our system
were not its sole components. Material rewards and opportunities for one's children were also important motives.
With affluence came the discovery that success, as a vali-
dating device, wore thin very soon. Material rewards were
no longer so significant. Opportunities for the coming generation were no longer scarce. The way of life of the
middle class changed. The children started in where the

parents left off. They did not have the same motivation. They saw their parents' lives as much less than successes. They began to question. The old, once ineradicable, unconscious assumptions began to be seen as problematic.

Speaking of the Calvinist, Weber had said,

The ascetic, when he wishes to act within the world, that is, to practice inner-worldly asceticism, must become afflicted with a sort of happy stupidity regarding any question about the meaning of the world, for he must not worry about such questions. Hence, it is no accident that inner-worldly asceticism reached its most consistent development on the foundation of the Calvinist God's absolute inexplicability, utter remoteness from every human criterion, and unsearchableness as to his motives. Thus, the inner-worldly ascetic is the recognized "man of vocation," who neither inquires about nor finds it necessary to inquire about the meaning of his actual practice of a vocation within the world, the total framework of which is not his responsibility but his God's. For him it suffices that, through his rational actions in this world, he is personally executing the will of God, which is unsearchable in its ultimate significance.[32]

The secularized Puritan ethic lost the theological framework which originally gave it meaning. But Calvinist man, conditioned not to question, failed to notice that the meaning had vanished. All his rationality was turned outward in manipulation of a world seen as pure object. All his energy was required to discipline himself and to do his job. He became the citizen of Harvey Cox's version of the secular city. He became, in Weber's words, a specialist without spirit and sensualist without heart. Of course, these are all caricatures. For within this citizen of the post-Christian middle class world, there stirred secret impulses and inchoate aspirations. These often formed themselves into visible phenomena on the fringes. Or they gave rise to leisure time avocations. But the basic structure of the system remained intact.

Yet, the radicalism of the thirties was more than a response to the depression. It was also the continuation of a native American tradition of left protest and of aspirations for a better and more humane society. From the utopians of Emerson's time, of which he said it seemed as if everyone had in his pocket a plan for a new society, to the post-Civil War agrarianism and populism, to the socialists of the 1900's, and to the so-called red decade of the thirties, a vigorous American tradition of dissent and of utopian aspiration is evident. "Call me Ishmael," began Melville in a work which certainly questioned the Anglo-American secularized "calling" of Ahab whose means are rational but whose end is, on his own admission, mad. Throughout the turbulent rise of American industrialism, the process which "established" the present "establishment," many Americans called themselves "Ishmael" in some hidden recesses of their souls. Sometimes the churches could talk to these people; some of them indeed were in the churches. But most of them were outside and out of real communication with those institutions which were the bearers of the Christian tradition. Much in the protest went back eventually to Christianity; much was descended from prophetic protest and evangelical aspiration. But it had now been transformed by the secularization of the Enlightenment and, in the more radical cases, by the reinterpretation of Marx.

In our day, all the processes we have looked at reach a

kind of culmination. The Industrial Revolution reaches fulfillment in a society in which inner-worldly asceticism without any theological or ontological justification becomes more and more absurd. Mass higher education brings large masses into contact with the critical thought of the past several centuries. Social mobility, assimilation to the general American culture and a loss of the older ethnic roots, and geographical mobility erode older, unconsciously accepted premises and allegiances. Rapid change makes any "settling down" and "retraditionalization" impossible. The breakdown of world order in two world wars and the existence of nuclear weapons reveal the flux under all things of which theoretical knowledge had already caught a glimpse. Yet, in the midst of this, the old system continues, continually modified, but without any basic changes. The autonomy of which Weber spoke remains characteristic of the core occupational system, and that system remains the core of American adult life.

Is there really any wonder that increasing numbers of youth find this situation absurd? They are not proving to themselves what their parents were proving. They are not rural boys come to town or immigrants' sons getting ahead and becoming American in the process. They are not the traditional industrial poor of the nineteenth century struggling for a fair day's wage and a measure of security. For them, college becomes a *collage;* a potpourri of the major ideas, the major criticisms, the major aspirations of Western man. Their elders evidently expected them to accept all this in the spirit of the parents' own cocktail hour culture and then become conventional adults in the old system. Fool around with ideas, but life must

be recognized as "serious"! Here seriousness refers to that
"happy stupidity" with which one is supposed to enter
unquestioningly into the "iron cage." The youth cannot
do it. They cannot help recoiling. Their structured historical and sociological situation has pried them loose
from the old contexts; that is why they "hang loose." What
thinkers have done in thought—to break through ethno-
centric and historically specific provincialism—history has
done for these youth. The social mobility of their families
and their own psychic mobility combine with the consequences of rapid change and the revolution in communications to make these youth feel unrelated to an historic
past.

Arthur Koestler, noting this characteristic in post-war
Europe, spoke of youth as being born "without navels."
Kenniston says that his alienated "see themselves as largely
ahistorical figures."[33] For college youth the "problem of
identity" has become a central one. To be thrust upon
the highly mobile scene without traditional moorings is
to have the question of what is it all about raised in a
profound way. That leads to an even more basic question:
What am I all about? Indeed, who am I?

These youth read Sartre and Camus, but they are psychologically conditioned to feel resonance with what they
find there. They know of Freud and Marx but their up-
rootedness from the past and from a stable and integrated
present social and cultural context has prepared them to
see readily what to Marx and Freud were exciting dis-
coveries. The iron cage is being rejected by these young
people; the "happy stupidity" of unquestioning performance is being discarded. The worth of conventional activity in work or elsewhere for its own sake, of conventional
competition in the occupational system to prove oneself

a man, of conventional getting ahead in the public world
as an assertion of belongingness—all these are hangovers
from an earlier period as far as many of these young
people are concerned. People "under thirty" seek another
way or would like to try to seek one.

There seems to be a crisis in what Marx called "the
epoch of the bourgeoisie." With that crisis, there is also
a crisis in its smug Enlightenment ideology. Today's dis-
senting youth do not assume on the authority of an
absurd society that religion has been proven obsolete for
all time by the mockers of the Enlightenment or their
more prosaic bourgeois descendents. These young people,
on the whole, do not understand religion. But they suspect
on the basis of their own life experience that there is
somewhere a realm that transcends the sphere of every-
dayness—of work, of huckstering, of war. They seek contact with such a realm. They secretly wish for a utopian
society, but they distrust all ideologies and utopias. However, they see the present organization of human life as
somehow basically wrongheaded. They reject, in short, the
complacent this-sidedness of middle class rationality. They
wish more than anything else for what we have called
an ontologically grounded sense of direction. They are
not, however, attuned to the language of tradition or the
churches.

The churches here face their greatest challenge. The old
Enlightenment bigotry is on the way out. Christianity
will be listened to. But does it have anything to say?
These youth, thoroughly confused by the contradictions
of their lives and the antinomies of their education, are
asking real questions. They are, it is true, often giving
regrettable, superficial and short-circuited answers to them.
They seek meaning; they seek it, to use their pet pejora-

tive term, outside the "establishment." Does Christianity have something to offer them? Can it first discover their wave length and then listen to them?

FOOTNOTES

1. See for example, *From Anathema to Dialogue: A Marxist Challenge to the Christian Churches*, Roger Garaudy, Luke O'Neill, tr. New York: Herder, 1966).

2. Cf. Harvey Cox, *The Secular City* (New York: Macmillan, 1965).

3. Joachim Wach, *Types of Religious Experience, Christian and Non-Christian* (Chicago: Chicago University Press, 1951), p. 32ff.

4. Cf. Martin Heidegger, *Being and Time*, John Macquarrie and Edward Robinson, tr. (New York: Harper, 1962).

5. Ludwig Feuerbach, *The Essence of Christianity*, George Eliot, tr. (New York: Peter Smith, 1957).

6. F. W. Nietzsche, *The Philosophy of Nietzsche* (New York: Modern Library, 1927).

7. Sigmund Freud, *The Future of An Illusion*, W. B. Robins-Scott, tr. (Garden City, New York: Doubleday, 1957); also *Civilization and Its Discontents*, James Strachey, ed. and tr. (New York: Norton, 1961).

8. Jean-Paul Sartre, *Being and Nothingness: An Essay on Phenomenological Ontology*, H. E. Barnes, tr. (New York: Citadel, 1956).

9. Albert Camus, *The Stranger* (New York: Knopf, 1946).

10. Kenneth Kenniston, *The Uncommitted: Alienated Youth in American Society* (New York: Harcourt, 1960), p. 176. Copyright © 1960, 1962, 1965 by Kenneth Kenniston. Reprinted by permission of Harcourt, Brace & World, Inc.

11. *Ibid.*, p. 179.

12. *Ibid.*, p. 180.

13. *Ibid.*, p. 181.

14. *Ibid.*, p. 182—italics in original

15. *Ibid.*, p. 183.

16. *Ibid.*, p. 184.

17. *Ibid.,* p. 190.

18. *Ibid.,* p. 192.

19. *Ibid.,* p. 196.

20. *Ibid.,* pp. 396–7.

21. J. L. Simmons and Barry Winograd, *It's Happening* (Santa Barbara, California: Marc-Laird, 1966), pp. 6 and 7 *et passim.*

22. Paul Goodman, *Growing Up Absurd* (New York: Random House, 1956), pp. 139, 144, 158.

23. Alec Vidler, *Modernist Movement in the Roman Church* (Cambridge University Press, 1934), pp. 15–16.

24. C. C. J. Webb, *A History of Philosophy* (London: Oxford University Press, 1915), p. 210.

25. Merle Curti, *The Growth of American Thought* (New York: Harper, 1943).

26. William Warren Sweet, *The American Churches* (New York: Abingdon, 1948), pp. 11–53, ("Left Wing Protestantism Triumphs in America").

27. Talcott Parsons, *The Social System* (Glencoe, Illinois: Macmillan (Free Press), 1951).

28. Max Weber, *The Protestant Ethic and the Spirit of Capitalism,* Talcott Parsons, tr. (New York: Scribner, 1948).

29. Kenneth Kenniston, *op. cit.,* pp. 396–7 (see footnote 20).

30. Paul Goodman, *op. cit.,* p. 158 (see footnote 22).

31. Simmons and Winograd, *op. cit.,* pp. 28–29.

32. Max Weber, *The Sociology of Religion,* Ephraim Fischoff, tr. (Boston, Massachusetts: Beacon Press, 1963).

33. Kenneth Kenniston, *op. cit.,* p. 202.

VI

The Real Challenge of Secularism

Admittedly it is a transgression of a disciplinary order for a sociologist to embark upon a diagnosis which involves also a modest attempt at prescription concerning the current religious crisis. Yet one may take consolation from the recognition that the severe problems of our day challenge a narrow professionalism to demonstrate that its knowledge and its know-how can be put to the service of man and the humanization of his societies and the general conditions of his life. Therefore I shall attempt to indicate one area where the process of secularization appears to me more of a threat than a promise, and to suggest at least some preliminary means of meeting the threat. I recognize that in any such attempt one's own personal perspective and values influence the salience given to various findings derived from more objective analysis.

SECULARIZATION AND THE LOSS OF RELIGIOUS FUNCTIONS

Religion performs a whole series of important functions for men and societies; and when religions are rendered obsolete by social and cultural change, these functions tend to be performed by other surrogate human activities and institutions, or they tend to be lost altogether. Undoubtedly many of the functions performed by religion historically in the West are now performed more or less adequately by other kinds of organizations and institutions, political parties and movements, universities, nations, etc. Religious men may feel that they detect an idolatrous element in some of these functional surrogates, but in many cases human needs may find more adequate satisfactions, and human aspirations more adequate expression in the newer social and cultural forms. Yet it seems that certain functions are lost, and this loss constitutes one of the most perilous aspects of the current religious crisis.

A sense of, a recognition of, and a response to transcendence has been the central attribute of Judaism and Christianity. We are all quite aware that at times, and indeed much too frequently, a penultimate ecclesiasticism in the church and a penultimate ethnic communalism in the synagogue tended to idolatrize these religions themselves, yet the central notion of transcendence was never lost. A relation to the transcendent remains the most important characteristic of biblical religion, affecting most profoundly the Western sense of time and history, of individual dignity and destiny, and even providing an important enabling factor for Western utilitarianism in its great accomplishments of technology. It has given Western man a "beyond" in relation to which he could develop identity as a person differentiated from his social milieu and achieve a manipulative leverage over the things of his situation and gain a tremendous mastery over them. It has enabled Western man to develop a sense of his own historicity, and has made it possible for him to de-myth-ologize, and thereby to secularize, important aspects of his view of the world and his place within it. From such developments came autonomous philosophy and objective science.

The ascendency and leverage achieved by Western men over their own historical situation are to be seen in the 18th and 19th centuries when men in Europe and America concerned themselves with the rational reconstruction of society, the forms of social relations, the status of women, the fundamental aims of education and the uses and abuses of technology and brought forth numerous criti-cisms of the existing order and proposals for radical change. Carl Becker, over thirty years ago, pointed out that the men of the Enlightenment inherited uncritically from their Christian ancestors a cosmic framework of order and rational intelligibility. Similarly, physiocrats, the early economists of both mercantilism and *laissez faire,* the utopian socialists, the reformers of prisons and asylums, the abolitionists, and finally the disciples of Marx, inherited from the Christian past a sufficient degree of transcendence over the press of social and historical imme-diacy to be capable of telling criticism and creative pro-posals pointing to a radical reorganization of current social conditions, and the projection of pathways to human ful-fillment in marked contrast to the institutions and con-ventions of the day.

In our day both these inheritances seem to have run out to an alarming degree. Our contemporaries do not generally see the cosmos through the secularized Chris-tian lenses of the Enlightenment, but rather tend to find confusion and absurdity characterizing man's place in his world. They rather feel the uncanny presence of a nihilism lurking beneath the surface, a nihilism that reflects simultaneously a greater knowledge of man's make-up and the conditions of his life than possessed by previous generations, and a loss of any ascendency and leverage making critical and rational choice possible with respect to the confusing array of human possibilities.

In such a situation the development of constructive programs of large scope and long range becomes impossible. Thus in our day we successfully conquer time and space with the instruments of our sophisticated technology, but we assume that the social structure of work is given for all time. We even come to dread the possibility of greatly increased leisure. We successfully fight against mortal disease and prolong human life up to and beyond the biblical three score years and ten for increasing numbers, but we are incapable of answering the most elementary problems of meaning either for the old or the young, except by resort to the conventional shibboleths inherited from a past whose premises we do not share and whose faith we do not believe. In the midst of technological wonders and scientific marvels, we seem unable to imagine any form of social organization that would go beyond the established disciplines and routines of production and the existing modes and channels of distribution. Emerson once said that in his day everyone seemed to have in his vest pocket a plan for the reorganization of society. In our day many of our youth have placards in their hands and aspirations in their hearts, but ideas and plans are in short supply whether in vest pockets or in human heads.

Although we today in the social sciences understand far more than any previous generation concerning the nature of social conditioning, the relations of men to groups, and the relation of human needs to situations, we are less able to diagnose disorders and prescribe remedies than our ancestors. Our most advanced current notion of social reform would seem to consist of proposals to enable the culturally deprived to become good middle class citizens—cogs in the established and unreformed apparatus of production and consumption. The very university itself, derived from the church and representing the hard-won independence of the mind from sacerdotal dominance, tends to settle into the role of government researcher, trainer of professional personnel, and contributor to what Maxim Gorky once called the embellishment of the boredom of bourgeoise life. It is not that we are without knowledge or for that matter without sensitivity, but where are we to find a relationship to any transcendent values enabling us to take a fundamentally critical position and on this basis to propose creative changes?

In the 19th century, Ludwig Feuerbach saw the God of the Jews and the Christians as the projection of man, the expression of obscure self-knowledge projected by men into the void. There it was made the object to which man attempted to relate himself, thereby making himself the object of his own projected, objectified self. In this way man became alienated from himself. To Feuerbach atheism meant the destruction of this harmful projection. Man would be liberated from his self-alienation; he would be made whole again. It is one of the curious ironies of our time that it has not quite worked out that way. The loss of belief in the transcendent God of his fathers left Western man caught in the confusions and relativities of his current situation, left him without a sense of direction, left him shorn of the basic conviction that he belongs in the world at all. Consequently, to escape his homelessness, he must often follow directions inherited from past convention, or accepted from present fashion, with less critical consideration than often displayed by his believing and orthodox ancestors.

THE ROLES OF RELIGION

Religion in the West with its sense of transcendence has traditionally been concerned with relation, celebration, and cultivation. It asserted that man is related to his world in other ways than by manipulation and control. It affirmed that he seeks an internal resonance with the structures and rhythms of his surroundings and through them with a transcendent beyond. What remains of this for secularized man is largely a matter of aesthetics. While that in itself is important, it is seriously to be doubted whether the aesthetic approach separated from every last shred of ontological grounding can do justice to the aesthetic realm iteslf. It certainly cannot make the aesthetic realm meaningful in any fruitful way for other areas of life. The arts do not under our present circumstances contribute notably to the evolution of an art of living.

Traditional religion saw in man's relation to nature and his fellow man an ethical dimension built into the very ontological structure of a divinely created cosmos. Today many of our contemporaries seek in an ethical experience a pathway to a meaningful non-utilitarian relationship to existence. Many seek religious epiphanies in ethically oriented or ethically interpreted movements of protest concerned with civil rights and foreign policy, but such behavior appears to be the product of the older traditions, as remnants of the old rather than harbingers of the new. Others seek in social and sexual experiment to achieve satisfactory fellowship and to evolve a design of ethical relationship. In the use of the new psychedelic drugs a new method is seized upon in the effort to find the peak experience once offered within the precincts of the mystical traditions. All these experimentations bear the marks of trial and error, at best but modestly influenced either by our great religious traditions or our impressive intellectual heritage.

The Hebraic sense of God's transcendence, whether in the Old or New Testament, contained two seemingly incompatible but actually intimately related elements. God was both wholly other, radically different than his creation and at the same time near to it and concerned with it. Transcendence involved immediacy. The loss of transcendence and immediacy with respect to the God of the Western tradition involved a loss of ascendency and leverage over the human situation for those whose faith, together with its unconscious precipitates, vanished with developing secularization. Men lost the ability to take genuine, long term initiative concerning social issues. In the realm of individual existence they have tended to abandon the search for the "good life," a central interest in Western philosophy from Socrates' time almost to our own.

Secondly, religion is concerned with celebration. Modern secularized observers have sometimes concluded that men turn to religion in times of defeat, misfortune, or frustration. While this is often the case, it is no less true that men also turn to religion to celebrate good fortune and to express joy. Suffering is not the only path to transcendence. Men celebrate success, victory, accomplishment, and enjoyment, and through them often find a breakthrough to the sacred powers beyond the appearances of their daily lives. Without such celebration the world of secularized man flattens out. He becomes fact-minded in Mannheim's pejorative sense. Justus Buchler has suggested that "Physics, history, and poetry are cognitive in different respects, not in different degrees." There are many aspects of our world besides those given primacy in the apprehensions of the problem-solving mentality and found useful for manipulation.

Human experience is in fact many-sided. Traditional religion tried to do justice to this fact through its celebrations, its special times and reasons, its places blessed and set apart, its elaborate liturgies, and its varied penitential observances and piacular rites. Thus it was able to proclaim not simply in words but in expressive action man's rich and many-sided relation to the world of his experience. Despite the great proliferation of art forms and the democratization of their availability, it can hardly be claimed that secular culture has produced functional equivalents to do justice to this varied character of human existence, let alone relate it to the fundamental problems of relation, meaning and destiny which confront men in our day.

Finally, religion in the West has been concerned with what has been called traditionally the "cure of souls." Religion traditionally, whether rightly or wrongly, not simply answered questions of meaning and destiny, but also provided criteria and methodology for the promotion and guidance of interior development. Christianity took over from classical philosophy the notion and *areté* of virtue as the fulfillment of the human potential. This conception, which was central to the Hellenic conception of man, grew over long centuries from the excellence of the Homeric warrior and Hesiodic peasant to the citizen's *areté* of Solon and Pericles, and finally to the philosopher's conception of self-realization in Plato and Aristotle. Philosophy, developing and reinterpreting the older conception, added the notion of *metanoia*, of consciously executed personal change.

In Christianity these two conceptions of *metanoia* and *areté*, of self-directed personal change of direction and systematic effort after self-realization, were understood in the light of the sayings of the Lord in the fifth, sixth, and seventh chapters of the Gospel of St. Matthew. The result, under the peculiar historical conditions of the time, was a monastic ideal finding expression in the monastic community. This conception remained for long the highest conception of evengelical perfection, first for monks, then for the secular clergy, and finally for the serious religious laity. The Reformation did not make any notable creative change here, but rather may be said to have propagated still further among laymen the monastic ideal but slightly reformed in its essential features. The notion of the ideal Christian man remained cast in a monkish mold, a fact that did not help Christians to adapt creatively to secularization.

I am not concerned here with an appraisal of this Christian interpretation and reworking of the Hellenic ideal, its adequacy to its own period or to ours. I am interested rather in the simple fact of its existence. Traditional religion was concerned and still is concerned with the realization of man's spiritual potential as it understands that potential, was and still is concerned with the cultivation of interiority, of personal depth, and in the formation of character after a model which was presumed to bring fulfillment and realization of self.

Today, with the vast contributions of the various

schools of psychoanalysis and analytic psychology, it might be thought that we are in a position to develop a more adequate model and propose more effective methods. Yet most of our accomplishments in this respect remain analytical. We are very good at undoing the distortions of development which life has brought about in those who volunteer to become patients of psychoanalysis, but we do little to advance man's general knowledge concerning what self-realization might be and to offer means of its achievement. Our psychologies are equipped for "cure" in the modern, not in the classical sense. If the loss of transcendence leaves us a mundane man without the leverage for long range initiative in changing society; if the loss of celebration leaves us with one-dimensional man based upon a highly developed problem-solving mentality, then the loss of any concern with serious personal responsibility for interior personal development in terms of our greatly increased knowledge leaves the whole matter of human realization to chance or to charlatanry.

It would appear that the notion of human development and self-realization has been left to amateurs when it has not been thought of as something that takes care of itself. In medical school, a man learns to be a doctor; in engineering school, an engineer; in the general graduate school of arts and science, a scholar or scientist; in the various occupations, training and work experience develop the desired traits. But all of these leave out serious consideration of the potential of human interiority and of the rounded fulfillment of the human capacities to be human.

What is suggested here is that three important functions of traditional religion deriving from its concern with relation, celebration and cultivation have tended progressively to be lost with the secularization of culture. Further, it is suggested that the most serious of these losses may be the third—the cultivation of human personality by self-conscious, rational, informed self-cultivation based upon a sophisticated model of human possibilities and a sophisticated tradition regarding the care of the human spirit. Secularism as the acceptance of the consequences of secularization as normative has failed utterly to concern itself with this realm and has either relegated it to traditional religion within the latter's own province or dismissed it as an outmoded concern. The result has been one-dimensional man; perspectival, professional man; fragmented, occupational man.

The shift in emphasis from the sacred to the profane and from an I-Thou to and I-It relation to the world has increased our emphasis upon external mastery and enhanced our capacity to manipulate and control the conditions of our lives. In this atmosphere human concerns in the humanities and the social sciences have become increasingly the objects of objectified methodologies. This has in fact enormously increased our knowledge, but it has also rendered the problems of the human relevance of our expanded knowledge increasingly difficult. One consequence has been the consigning of the problems of human cultivation to the realm of "emotion" seen as "gut-reaction" and removed from rational criticism or supervision. We have all but abandoned the attempt to cultivate and develop human personality in terms of an informed model and an intelligent set of procedures. Only in the church have such concerns remained important. But the secularization of culture and the accompanying decline in the importance of organized religion has tended to render the church less and less capable of acting in such matters for large numbers of people.

Is, then, this important function simply to be allowed to lapse through default? We have become capable of blowing up the earth; we are about to visit the moon; but we have to a shockingly large extent lost the sense of responsibility for human fulfillment understood as interior development and not simply exterior adjustment. It is not simply that secularism has lost the sense of what Christianity means by grace, a concept that may indeed have secular equivalents worth seeking. It has ceased even to be intelligently and sensibly Pelagian.

In these circumstances I would suggest that Jews and Christians have more important concerns than their reciprocal conflicts and confusions. They must concern themselves with the future of mankind. Whatever the poignancy of memories of past conflicts, that past is becoming obsolete. As the bearers of Western religion, there are more serious concerns before us.

Concluding Unscientific Postscript

To rediscover the relevance of his heritage, man must achieve authentic transcendence and genuine community. Institutionalized religion must contribute to this goal to the best of its capacity. To be relevant today, religion must translate into a contemporary idiom the "foolishness of the cross." By synthesizing joy and tragedy in a new way, man could become at home in his world, even while remaining forever a sojourner and a pilgrim in the midst of his fondest, this-worldly achievement and values. Religion must nourish and sustain an interiority that makes external relationship and accomplishment possible. But this interiority must never lose itself in its products; it must be able to find its own way among the many ways it creates in the world. To be relevant today, religion must support those human aspirations that cry for fulfillment in terms of the modern technological capacity. It must become relevant to the effort toward a more abundant life for man. It must teach not only the appropriateness of justice, wisdom, fortitude, and courage, but it must also bear witness to a faith, hope, and charity rendered relevant to the new world man has made and the new man whose promise it contains. Institutionalized religion and institutionalized learning must strive to beget honesty and transmit seriousness in facing problems, eschewing fixated ideologies and petty interests. Then, spirit and reason will find their own embodiment, for one may still hope that the spirit bloweth where it listeth. Let men learn, in the words of Dag Hammarskjold, to become recipients out of humility and to be grateful for being allowed to listen, observe, and understand.